# GUITAR PLAYER'S
# NOTEBOOK

## MUSIC THEORY AND MANUSCRIPT PAPER
## FOR CREATIVE GUITARISTS

JUSTIN S. DAVIS

WARD STREET PRESS . SEATTLE . 2016

*Guitar Player's Notebook*

info@wardstreetpress.com

If not available at your local bookstore, this book may be ordered from numerous online distributors. For additional information about this book and about Ward Street Press, visit our web site at:

http://www.wardstreetpress.com

For additional information about Justin S. Davis and the *Guitar Player's Notebook*, visit Justin's web sites at:

http://www.justinsdavis.com        or        http://www.guitarplayersnotebook.com


*Guitar Player's Notebook*

ISBN: 978-0-9887417-4-4

**ACKNOWLEDGMENTS**

I'd like to extend my thanks to Vee Sawyer for her contributions of art and photography, and for designing the layout of this book. It was Vee's idea to have a blank template page that could be quickly filled in during a lesson to document the material covered, and her husband John Budz was the first of my students to benefit from her concept. Thanks as well to John Budz for his text and layout editing, and his patient encouragement for me to see this project through to completion. I want to thank my student Angela Lucioni for reading through the book and helping identify sections that needed additional editing. Special thanks to my friend and colleague Bob Crow for going above and beyond with his thorough review of the musical examples, and in offering so many useful, way too good to ignore, editorial suggestions. And finally I want to extend my deepest gratitude to my wife Shane for her constant love and support through this project, and all the other projects too. I love you.

For Hannah.

# TABLE OF CONTENTS

# INTRODUCTION

I think it is important to state here at the beginning that I don't believe music has rules.

Guitarists are famous for being rule averse. Many of us begin as self-taught players, learning by ear in a way that many other instrumentalists can't imagine. And it's that reluctance to formal development that gives us the reputation we have. There is a well-deserved old joke that claims putting sheet music in front of a guitar player is the surest way to get them to turn the volume down. I know many players who have no interest in learning how to read music or about music theory. Some of them defend their position with a claim that learning the more academic structure of music will inhibit them creatively.

I agree that it is desirable to strive for and nurture maximum creative freedom. Musicians, and guitarists in particular, are often well served by breaking traditions and embracing fearlessness in both composition and improvisation.

I absolutely reject, however, the argument that learning music fundamentals like sight-reading and theory is a hindrance to that freedom. Rather, I have found over and over in my career as a performer, songwriter, and teacher that sharing a vocabulary common amongst musicians has far more benefits than costs.

No single thing aided my progress as a guitarist more than learning to read music. I gained through the process an understanding of the layout of the instrument, an ability to recognize patterns on the fingerboard, and to make instant connections between scales and chords. I developed an ability to communicate with precision with other musicians.

I learned through studying music theory to understand harmonic tendencies. That awareness has helped me quickly learn songs by ear, to anticipate and hear chord changes before they happen, and to develop confidence and fluency soloing over chord progressions and harmonizing melodies.

I push all of my students to learn to read and write music, and to learn the fundamentals of music theory. And unsurprisingly, through their study they make the same leaps forward in their musicianship that I did. The rapid progress my students make continually proves that the effort they put into learning these musical tools pays huge dividends.

Which brings me to the *Guitar Player's Notebook*. I developed this notebook for use in my studio, and it contains the diagrams and explanatory content I consider the most foundationally important for my students: an outline of the basics of music notation, the circle of fifths, scale construction and visualization strategies, and much more.

This notebook is not a traditional method of how to play guitar. Rather, this is intended to serve as a valuable supplement to any student's lesson material, and provide motivated guitarists and songwriters with a short and easily digestible resource to help fill in some potential gaps in their understanding of music's underlying architecture.

The *Guitar Player's Notebook* contains two books in one. The crash course in theory provided at the beginning is followed by a set of blank notation template pages, conceived to be a useful tool for note taking during guitar lessons.

Most private guitar lessons run between thirty minutes to an hour, once a week. While there is an obvious need to provide some written record of each lesson to help ensure success in the week of practice, there is simply not a lot of time to spend writing things down.

I spent a year using these template pages with my students, refining the layout to maximize the efficacy of the layout and my efficiency in notating lessons. Although there are numerous books available (many of which I've used) that provide various combinations of the notational elements found here, this layout satisfies my needs as a teacher in a way that no other notebook has.

I'm thrilled with how this book turned out — so much so that I felt it was worth sharing beyond my private studio. Best wishes with your guitar playing!

*Justin S. Davis*
*Seattle, Washington*

# ELEMENTS OF NOTATION

## GUITAR SPECIFIC NOTATION

Several notation marks are unique to guitar music. In this section, we will run through those that are most common and important. Understanding these markings now will help you to play the examples that follow in the later sections of this book.

## STRINGS

Numbers with circles around them refer to specific strings. For example, the number ⑥ represents the sixth string, the lowest pitch string, while the number ① represents the first string, the highest pitched string.

Remember, we always use the words "low" and "high" to describe the *sound* of a note, not the note's physical position on the guitar. The open sixth string is the lowest note you can play on the instrument, so the sixth string is the "low" string, despite the fact that the sixth string is further from the floor than the first string.

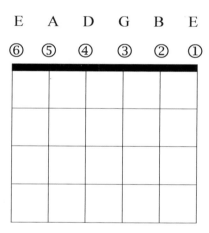

## PICK DIRECTIONS

⊓ = **Downstroke** (strum or pluck towards the floor)

V = **Upstroke** (strum or pluck towards the ceiling)

## FINGERS

The fingers on your **left hand** are labeled 1, 2, 3, and 4, starting from the index finger. The left hand thumb is labeled with a T.

**Right hand** fingers, starting from the thumb, are labeled *p, i, m, a.*

The pinky of the right hand is very seldom used and has no standard name. I've seen it marked as *c*, *x*, or *q*, but I've not seen it marked at all outside of flamenco music, so we'll ignore it here.

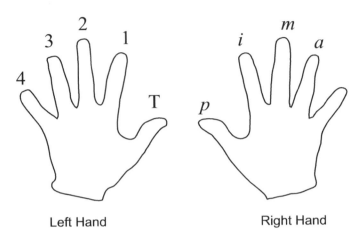

Left Hand                 Right Hand

---

Why *p, i, m, a*? Those are the first letters of the Spanish words for the fingers, and the guitar is originally a Spanish instrument. The guitar is popular worldwide, but the Spanish abbreviations *p i m a* are still the standard in guitar notation.

thumb = *pulgar*
index = *indice*
middle = *medio*
ring = *anular*

---

## POSITION

A guitar position is named after the fret your 1st finger plays. Each of your other fingers get their own frets going up sequentially from the first finger. For example, if you are playing in **first position**, then your 1st finger is on the first fret, your 2nd finger is on the second fret, 3rd finger, third fret, and so on.

Quick! If your 3rd finger is on the seventh fret, what position are you in?

If you said 5th position, you've got it!

Positions are marked in guitar music by **Roman numerals**.

Here is a scale example that uses three of the notational marks we've discussed so far: string marks, left hand fingerings, and position marks.

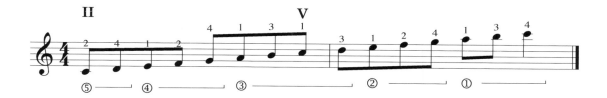

Even if you don't yet know how to read music, you should be able to use the notation marks to play this example. Let's break down how.

As we've already learned, the numbers with circles around them tell you what string the notes are on.

The numbers *without* circles specify which left hand fingers to use within the position. In this example, we begin in **second position** (marked by the Roman numeral **II** at the beginning of the example). Following all these instructions, the first note we play should be on the fifth string, with the second (middle) finger on the third fret. Be sure you try this on your guitar.

Midway through the example, we shift to **fifth position** on the third string. The last note is played on the eighth fret of the first string with the fourth (pinky) finger.

The example below is that same major scale with some additional notation callouts for clarity. Make sure you can play this scale and understand the notation elements before continuing in this book.

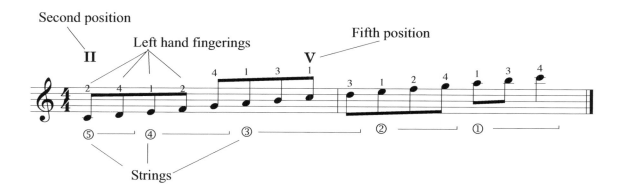

## FRETBOARD BOXES

Fretboard boxes are grids that provide a visual representation of the guitar fretboard. These are most commonly used to notate chord fingerings.

An X above the box tells you not to play that string, while an O above the box indicates that you need to let that string ring open. Left hand fingers are notated below the box or in the box next to the dots that represent the fingers.

The examples below use chord boxes to show you how to play three common chords, a G chord, a C chord, and a D chord. Play these chords on your guitar.

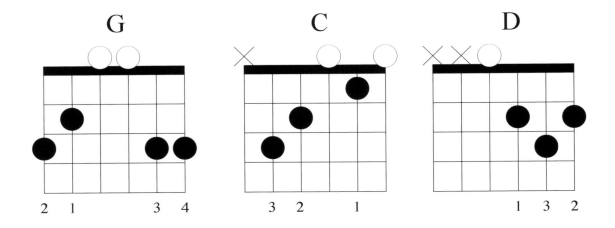

Fretboard boxes are also valuable tools for notating scale fingerings.

## E Blues Scale

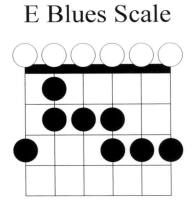

E Blues Scale, standard notation

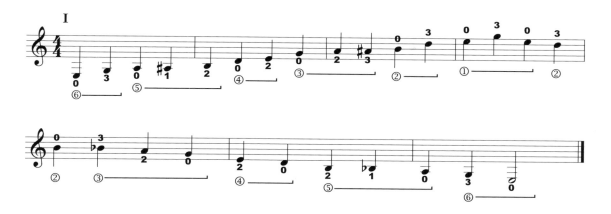

When compared with the same scale written in standard notation, the obvious advantage of the fretboard box is how much less space is required to convey information. Perhaps more importantly, however, the non-linear presentation of the notes in a fretboard box encourages players to find patterns and shapes in the notes, rather than just playing the notes in order, as described in standard notation. The different and unique patterns that students can discover by exploring scale fingerings are the first building blocks of improvisation, an essential skill all guitarists need to develop.

Play through the E blues scale using both the standard notation and the fretboard box as guides. Be sure you understand how to use both of these notational systems.

# Tablature (TAB)

Tablature, or **TAB** as it is commonly known, is a style of notation that dates from the 14th century and is currently the most common way to see guitar music published. As such, all guitar players need to know how to read and understand TAB.

In its modern form, TAB for guitar players is written on a six line staff. Each line represents a string of the guitar, the lowest line is the sixth string, and the top line is the first string.

Numbers are placed on the lines to indicate what fret to play. For example, a 3 on the second line down from the top is played on the third fret on the second string.

Just so you can play through a simple example of TAB notation, here is a familiar melody as it appears in TAB. Name that tune!

TAB is nearly ubiquitous in transcriptions of guitar music these days, and all guitar players should have familiarity with it. It is a demonstrably easier system for beginning guitarists to read than standard notation. Unfortunately, because it is found everywhere and is so easy to read, many guitar players never learn standard notation at all.

The ability to understand standard notation is essential for a complete musician. As a notational device, it conveys much more information than does TAB — not least of all a good picture of melodic contour — and guitarists who learn to read standard notation tend to have much better overall knowledge of their instrument. The vocabulary of music theory is based in standard notation, and it is the language that nearly all other musicians rely on. While I'll concede that TAB as a tool isn't going away, and that it is useful for guitarists to be able to read it, I cannot overstate my belief in the value and importance of learning to read standard notation. As such, the remainder of this book will use TAB staves sparingly and focus instead on getting you familiar with standard notation.

# FUNDAMENTALS OF STANDARD NOTATION

In this section, we're going to quickly run through the vocabulary of standard music notation. New terms throughout this book will be defined as they're introduced, but the terms listed here are among the most basic and common. These terms should be memorized before you go on to the rest of the book in order to avoid confusion up ahead. If you have taken any music classes at all, many of these terms will be familiar. If that is the case, take this as an opportunity to review. If not, let's get to work!

## THE STAFF

The staff is the five **lines** and four **spaces** on which music is written.

## CLEF

A clef is the symbol at the beginning of a staff that gives the staff its identity. There are two common clefs, the **treble clef** and the **bass clef**. Each clef is used to determine the pitch names on the staff. Our principle concern as guitarists is with the treble clef.

**The treble clef.** This is the clef that guitarists read. It's a stylized letter G. The lower curl of the clef wraps around the second line of the staff, making that line a G. Sometimes also called a G clef.

**The bass clef.** This is the clef that bass guitarists read. It's a stylized letter F. The two dots on either side of the fourth line of the staff make that line an F. Sometimes also called an F Clef.

**The Grand Staff**

A good way to see how these two clefs affect a staff is by looking at a **grand staff**. Essentially two staves linked together, a grand staff usually has a bass clef on the bottom stave and a treble clef on top. Guitarists don't read music on a grand staff (pianists do), but it provides a helpful visual of the two clefs in action.

Notice that the letters repeat themselves in alphabetical order every seven notes. That is the **musical alphabet**: A B C D E F G, over and over again. The distance between one note and another of the same letter name is an **octave**.

On the grand staff example below, you see that the note names of each staff are different (the bottom line on the bass clef is a G, while the bottom line of the treble clef is an E). Notice, however, that the musical alphabet climbs steadily between the two staves. The C note in the middle, known as "middle C", acts as the connecting note between the two staves and two clefs.

**Middle C** is shown twice, as it appears on each staff, but middle C is the same pitch and would be played on the same fret of your guitar, or with the same key of a piano, regardless of clef.

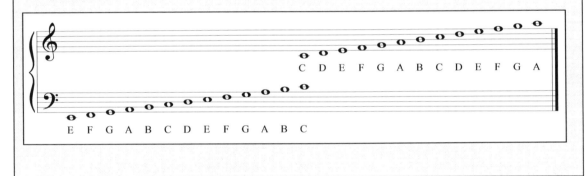

# NOTES ON A TREBLE CLEF STAFF

Guitarists almost exclusively use the treble clef, so examples from here on will all be written on treble clef staves.

Music on a staff is sound plotted on a graph. The lower a pitch sounds, the lower it appears on the staff. Likewise, the higher a pitch sounds, the higher on the staff the note is placed. As you can see in the grand staff example above, each of the five **lines** and four **spaces** of the staff represents a musical pitch:

The common mnemonic device to remember the names of the lines in a treble clef staff is: **Every Good Boy Does Fine.**

Every          Good          Boy          Does          Fine

The names of the four spaces are even easier to remember as they simply spell **FACE**.

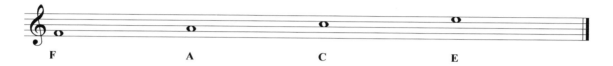

F                    A                    C                    E

For obvious reasons, the sooner you memorize these names and stop using the mnemonic, the faster and more easily you'll be able to read music.

Practice your recognition of note names by filling in the blanks in the exercise below. The first two are done for you.

B    G

# Ledger Lines

Notes that are too high or too low to be written on the staff are represented by ledger lines. Below we see ledger lines used to show the notes that extended beyond the staff, revealing the rest of the standard range of a 22-fret electric guitar.

E   F   G   A   B   C   D   G   A   B   C   D   E   F   G   A   B   C   D

Practice your recognition of the ledger line notes below the staff by filling in note names in the blanks for the exercise below. The first two are done for you.

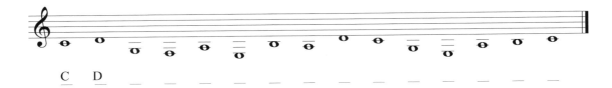

C     D

And now the same thing for the ledger lines above the staff:

C     D

## Ottava

**Ottava** is the Italian word for octave. The ottava mark ($8^{va}$) is an instruction to play notes, contained within the dashed line that follows the mark, an octave higher than written. If a section of music requires a lot of ledger line reading, an ottava mark can be used to simplify the task.

In the example below, we see the benefit of the ottava mark. The first measure shows pitches expressed with ledger lines. The second measure is exactly the same as the first, but the reading is simplified by the use of an ottava mark.

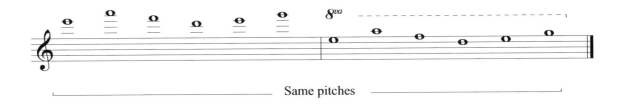

Same pitches

## Sharps, Flats, and Naturals

A **sharp** (♯) raises any note by one **half step** (the distance of one fret), while a **flat** (♭) lowers any note one half step. A **natural sign** (♮) is used to remove a previously assigned sharp or flat. Here is an example in fourth position you can (and should) play to hear the differences.

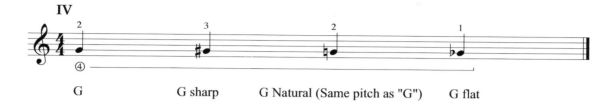

G                          G sharp        G Natural (Same pitch as "G")        G flat

Sharps and flats come into play in notation in two ways:

- As **accidentals**: when a note is altered for the duration of only one measure at a time, and only for the octave in which the note is written.

- In a **key signature**: when the note is altered for the entire section, across all octaves.

This is explained in more detail in the *Key Signatures* section on page 44.

There are two other, less common, accidentals you need to know. The **double sharp** (×) raises a note by two half steps. A **double flat** (♭♭) lowers a note by two half steps.

# Measures and Bar Lines

On the staff, **bar lines** mark the boundaries of **measures**, and measures contain groups of **beats**, which are the basic pulse of music.

The first beat of every measure is accented. For example, in measures consisting of 4 beats each, you would count **"ONE** two three four", with an accent on the first beat, the "one".

Various types of bar lines are used to mark measures, all of which are shown below:

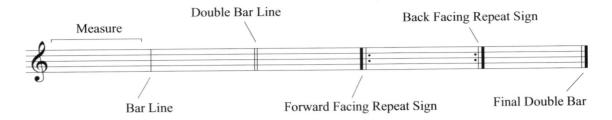

A single **bar line** is the most common and simply marks the ends of each measure. A **double bar line** marks the end of a section of music. The double bar with a heavy second line is the **final double bar** and marks the end of the song.

**Repeat signs** look similar to final double bars, but with the addition of two dots on either side of the middle staff line. Repeat signs are used to tell a musician to play the music between the repeats a second time, before moving on to the next part of the music.

Occasionally you will see only the back facing repeat sign, without the front facing one. When you see that, return to the beginning of the piece and play everything again.

Repeats will be discussed in more detail in the *Form* section on page 25.

## TIME SIGNATURES

The number of beats that fit into a measure is determined by the **time signature**. The time signature looks like a fraction at the beginning of a piece of music. The top number tells you how many beats will be in each measure, and the bottom number tells you what note value will be used to count the beats.

How many beats per measure (in this case, four)

What note value is counted as the beat (in this case, quarter notes)

Here are examples of some of the most common time signatures:

## RHYTHM

Rhythm is counted in **beats**, which are the basic pulse of music. Sounds are expressed as **notes**, while silences are written in **rests**. The following chart shows the most common notes, related rests, and their respective beat counts.

| Name | Duration | Note Symbol | Rest Symbol |
|---|---|---|---|
| Whole Note / Rest | 4 beats | 𝅝 | ▬ |
| Half Note / Rest | 2 beats | 𝅗𝅥 | ▬ |
| Quarter Note / Rest | 1 beat | ♩ | 𝄽 |
| Eighth Note / Rest | 1/2 beat | ♪ | 𝄾 |
| Sixteenth Note / Rest | 1/4 beat | 𝅘𝅥𝅯 | 𝄿 |

## STEMS, FLAGS, AND BEAMS

**Stems, Flags, and Beams**

All rhythmic notes (except for whole notes) have **stems** extending from their **note heads**.

Eighth, sixteenth, and shorter note values are also marked with **flags** hanging from their stems. When two or more of these flagged notes are part of the same beat, the flags are replaced with **beams**.

The location of a note head on the staff dictates the pitch of the note, but the stems and flags — along with the characteristics of the note head (solid, like a quarter note, or hollow like a half note) — give the note its rhythmic value.

In notation of a single melodic line, the rule is: notes below the middle line of the staff have their stems up, while notes from the middle line up have their stems facing down. When notes are beamed together, the note that is furthest from the middle line determines the stem direction of the group.

The reason the stems go up for lower notes, and down for lower notes, is to keep as much of the rhythmic information within the staff as possible. This makes sight-reading easier because the eye only has to track along the staff. Stem direction does not affect the pitch of the note.

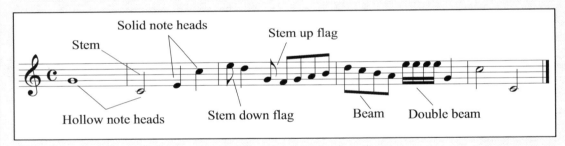

Guitars can play more than one line at a time, so when reading music with two or more **voices** (separate melodic lines) the stem direction will stay consistent with each voice. The top voice will have all its stems facing up, and the lower voice will have all its stems facing down.

Rhythms are counted out like so: a **whole note** lasts four beats, **half notes** last 2 beats, **quarter notes** are one beat each. **Eighth notes** are a half beat each, counted $1 + 2 +$ (spoken: one and, two and…) and **sixteenth notes** are counted 1 e + a 2 e + a (spoken: one ee and ah, two ee and ah…)

Write in the counts in the examples below. Mark rests by writing the beat, or beats, in parentheses. The first one is done for you as an example.

Practice playing and reading all rhythm exercises aloud to increase your comfort and fluency with written rhythms. Look also at any other sheet music you can get your hands on as a potential source for rhythm exercises. You cannot practice your rhythm too much!

## SYNCOPATION

Some rhythms emphasize weak beats by displacing the regular metrical accents. This is called **syncopation**.

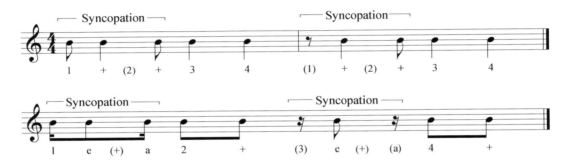

In the example above, the first quarter note lands on the *and* of beat one, shifting the accent away from beat two. Example two is the same principle as example one, but using smaller rhythmic units; sixteenth notes instead of eighth notes. Syncopation like this is a common feature of modern music, so it's important to learn to recognize it.

Write in the counts under the following example and mark the syncopated rhythms.

## DOTTED RHYTHMS

A dot placed after a note adds one half of that note's time value. For example, a dotted half note lasts three beats: the half note is two beats, the dot adds another half (half of two is one), and two plus one is three.

Dotted half note: ♩. = ♩ + ♩

| Name and Formula | Duration | Note Symbol | Rest Symbol |
|---|---|---|---|
| Dotted Whole Note / Rest<br>o + ♩ | 6 beats | o· | ▬· |
| Dotted Half Note / Rest<br>♩ + ♩ | 3 beats | ♩· | ▬· |
| Dotted Quarter Note / Rest<br>♩ + ♪ | 1-1/2 beats | ♩· | 𝄽· |
| Dotted Eighth Note / Rest<br>♪ + ♫ | 3/4 beat | ♪· | 𝄾· |
| Dotted Sixteenth Note / Rest<br>♬ + ♬ | 3/8 beat | ♬· | 𝄿· |

1  (2)  +  3  (4)    1   2   3  (4)  +    1  (2)  +  (3)  4    1  a  2  e  3  (4)  +

Rhythms can also be "double dotted," which adds to the half value of the first dot another quarter value, or half the value of the first dot.

Double dotted half note: ♩.. = ♩ + ♩ + ♪

## TRIPLETS

A division of a beat into three equal parts is called a triplet.

| Name | Duration | Notes Played | Note Symbol |
|---|---|---|---|
| Quarter note triplet | 2 beats | 3 notes | |
| Eighth note triplet | 1 beat | 3 notes | |
| Sixteenth note triplet | 1 beat | 6 notes | |

Eighth note triplets are counted: "one and uh, two and uh" as in the following example. The placement of the beat is shown below the triplets.

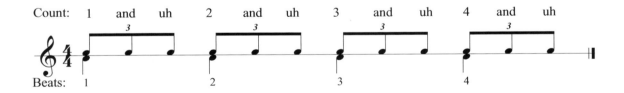

Quarter note triplets are easiest to understand in the context of the more common eighth note triples. Here is how they fit together.

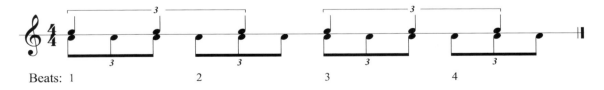

## TIES

A **tie** is the curved line that links two notes of the same pitch. You play the first of the two notes, but sustain through the full value of both rhythmic units without rearticulating the second note. Ties can occur across bar lines and inside single measures.

If the duration of a note lasts longer than the number of beats in a measure, you need to tie the last played note in the first measure to the appropriate value across the bar line to the following measure. For example, in 4/4 time, a note that lasts 5 beats would be written this way:

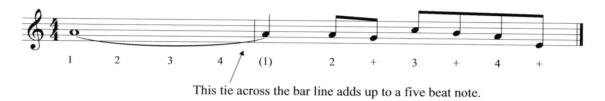

This tie across the bar line adds up to a five beat note.

Another typical example of a tie across the bar line could look like this:

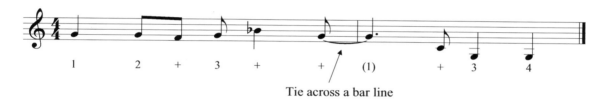

Tie across a bar line

Ties are not used only to cross bar lines. Often they are used to make rhythmic structures easier to read inside measures. For example, music written in common time (4/4) has a secondary stress on beat three, so notes that are sustained between beats two and three are often written with a tie. In this case it's a tie across the imaginary bar line splitting the measure in half.

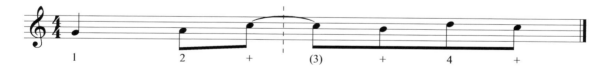

Ties are also often used between regular beats, like in the example below. The function in these cases is to show each beat in a measure in the clearest way possible.

## ARTICULATIONS

Written music has many symbols that indicate how a given note or phrase is to be played. These symbols are known as **articulations**. Here is a brief run down of the most common articulations guitar players see and use.

**Accent:** The downbeat (beat one) of each new measure is typically stressed. But if you want to put a stress on a different beat within the measure, you need to use an accent mark.

Accent

**Fermata:** A fermata, sometimes called a "birds-eye", marks a hold or pause, and can be placed over either a note or rest.

Fermata

**Staccato:** A note with a dot on top of it is to be played staccato, meaning very short. The note should be cut off immediately after it's played.

Staccato

**Slide:** While holding string down, you can slide your finger up or down, to or from, a given note. This is indicated by a dash showing the direction the slide should go, and whether your slide into the pitch or away from it.

Slide up to the note          Slide down from the note

**Slur:** A slur is marked with a curved line that looks somewhat similar to a tie, but instead of being two of the same pitches, a slur joins two or more *different notes*. On the guitar, the first of these notes would be plucked by the right hand, and the others would be sounded with either "hammer-ons" or "pull-offs", using the left hand only.

This example shows a lick with five pull-off type slurs:

Another typical way you will see and write slurs is as in this figure:

Only the first of these four notes is plucked with the right hand.
The rest are played using the left hand only, with hammer-ons and pull-offs.

Extended phrases played with slurs on the guitar are called **legato** (meaning "connected") phrases.

The difference between a tie and a slur is plain to see. Just remember: if the two notes are the same pitch it's a tie, if different, a slur.

Tie                                    Slur

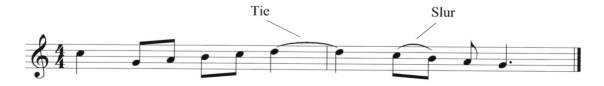

**Trill:** Trills are usually played by a quick series of hammer-ons and pull offs (although they can also be played across two strings) between the written note and the next higher scale note, and usually starting with the higher note.

Trill

**Tremolo:** A note that's marked tremolo is played repeatedly, as either even $32^{nd}$ notes or $16^{th}$ notes, depending on the tempo.

16th note tremolo          32nd note tremolo

**Vibrato:** A subtle shake of the note made by pushing and pulling a string or wiggling the tremolo or "whammy" bar.

Vibrato

## Slash Mark Notation

There are many different notation systems used in guitar music, particularly in the transcription of rhythm parts. One of the more common ways to notate rhythms is with **slash marks**.

Dmin7                    G7                    Cmaj7

Interpretation of this kind of slash mark notation varies with context. In a big band jazz setting, slashes are usually played as quarter notes using downstrokes. In other settings, in a rock band or a small jazz combo for instance, these slashes simply show where the chord changes are, and the player is free to improvise an appropriate rhythm pattern. In either situation, the guitarist is free to choose an acceptable chord voicing.

Many times, if a particular strumming pattern isn't required, the chord names will just be written inside the measures:

When a specific rhythm *is* needed, rhythmic slashes are used as in the following example. The upstroke/downstroke strumming directions are not always included, but are often helpful. The rhythm can be shown in the staff like in the example below or above the staff.

## Form

Musicians often refer to learning the **form** of a piece. Most music has sections of repeated material, and as a way to cut down on the time and space required writing it down, a number of shortcuts have been developed. When you're learning the form of a piece, what you're really doing is looking ahead through the music, tracking all the marks and repeats, and identifying the sections. Here are the most common signs to watch for.

- **Repeat Signs**: We looked at repeat signs earlier in the section on bar lines. This is the simplest and most common way to indicate repeated material.

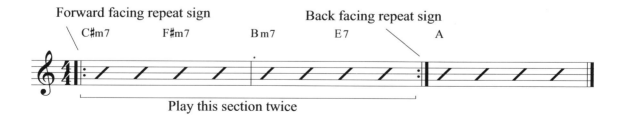

- **Simile Marks:** The next examples show the use of simile marks. These marks tell the performer to repeat the previous measure:

A **double simile mark** instructs the performer to repeat the previous two measures:

The pick directions shown above the rhythm slashes are editorial. They can be helpful to a performer, but are unnecessary for documenting rhythm.

- **D.C.** or **Da Capo**: Italian for *from the head*, the D.C. is a direction to return to the beginning of the piece. The second time through after a D.C. ignore any repeat signs you played the first time, unless otherwise indicated.

The example below, besides showing a simple D.C. form, also makes use of a **fine** mark. Fine (pronounced fee-nay) signals the end of the piece. This is typically only used if the end of the piece is somewhere other than the last written measure of the music. The instruction in the piece (D.C. al Fine) translates to: return to the beginning, and play to the end.

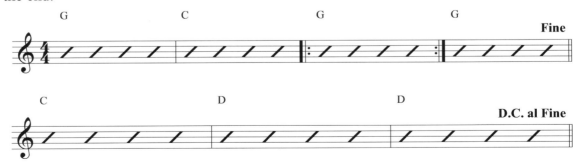

**Note**: Be sure you understand why the above example is 12 measures long.

- **D.S.** or Dal Segno: Italian for *from the sign*, D.S. is a direction to repeat from the sign or *segno* (𝄋). This works the same way as the D.C. form; any internal repeat signs are ignored during the D.S. repeat.

- **Coda**: When you see the direction "al coda" or "to coda", it's directing the performer to skip to the end section, marked with the coda symbol (⊕). A coda is a closing passage of music.

**Important:** Be sure to ignore both the D.S. and the To Coda marks the first time through. Those only become relevant *after* the "D.S. al Coda" instruction.

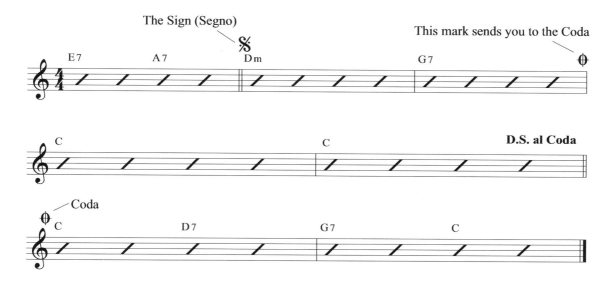

**Note**: Be sure you understand why this is a nine-measure example

- **First and Second Endings**

This is a way to have repeated material end in different ways. With this type of repeat, the performer takes the repeat under the first ending (marked under a bracket with a 1), but the second time through, the performer skips over the first ending measure and jumps instead to the second ending (under bracket 2).

**Note**: Be sure you understand that this example is eight measures long.

# NOTES ON THE FRETBOARD

These are the locations of the "natural" notes on the guitar fretboard. Any of these notes can become "sharp" (♯) by being fretted one half step (the distance of one fret) higher. Likewise, any note can be made "flat" (♭) by being fretted one half step (one fret) lower.

C♯, for example, can be played on the second fret of the second string, one fret higher than the C on that same string.

D♭ is played in the same place as C♯, the second fret of the second string, one fret lower than the D on the third fret.

Notes that are played in the same place but with different note names (like C♯ and D♭) are called **enharmonic equivalents**, which means that despite the different letter names, the two notes sound exactly the same.

The notes along the twelfth fret are the same as the notes of the open strings. This is because the twelve frets of each string complete an octave. The same pattern of notes repeats itself at the twelfth fret. In other words, the note names along the first fret are the same as the note names of thirteenth fret, just one octave higher. Likewise, the note names along the third fret are the same as the names of the notes of the fifteenth fret, and so on.

| | ⑥ E | ⑤ A | ④ D | ③ G | ② B | ① E |
|---|---|---|---|---|---|---|
| I | F | | | | C | F |
| | | B | E | A | | |
| III | G | C | F | | D | G |
| | | | | B | | |
| V | A | D | G | C | E | A |
| | | | | | F | |
| VII | B | E | A | D | | B |
| | C | F | | G | | C |
| IX | | | B | E | | |
| | D | G | C | F | A | D |
| | | | | | | |
| XII | E | A | D | G | B | E |

# BASIC ELEMENTS OF THEORY

## INTERVALS

We name the distance between two notes by its **interval**. Two notes of the same pitch are called **unisons**, while notes that are a half step apart are **minor seconds**, and so on. Here is a table to help you learn all the intervals within an octave.

| Unison | The same pitch |
|---|---|
| **Minor Second** | 1 half step distance |
| **Major Second** | 2 half step distance |
| **Minor Third** | 3 half step distance |
| **Major Third** | 4 half step distance |
| **Perfect Fourth** | 5 half step distance |
| **Tritone** (also called an **Augmented Fourth** or **Diminished Fifth**) | 6 half step distance |
| **Perfect Fifth** | 7 half step distance |
| **Minor Sixth** | 8 half step distance |
| **Major Sixth** | 9 half step distance |
| **Minor Seventh** | 10 half step distance |
| **Major Seventh** | 11 half step distance |
| **Octave** | 12 half step distance |

The best way to learn and understand the differences between these intervals is by hearing them.

Play the intervals along the length of one string. Each fret of the guitar is a half step, so if we count intervals along the fourth string for example, we get this:

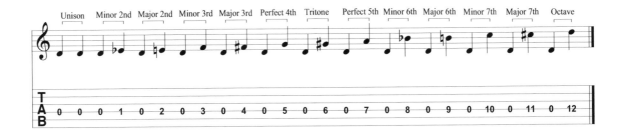

In this example you can see (and if you're playing the example like I hope you are, you can hear) the difference between the three-half step distance of a minor third and the four-half step distance of a major third. The TAB notation here is useful because the fret numbers double as a count of the half steps.

A **tritone** is the name given to the intervals of the **diminished fifth** (a half step smaller than a perfect fifth) and the **augmented fourth** (a half step larger than a perfect fourth). These intervals are **enharmonic equivalents**, meaning, despite having different names, the pitches are the same. The name tritone comes from the fact that the notes are the distance of three whole steps (6 half steps) apart. It is the midpoint division of a **chromatic** (a scale consisting of 12 notes, all half step intervals) **octave**.

Single string knowledge of intervals is useful, but not terribly practical for playing chords or most scales. On the following pages are charts outlining the intervals within an octave as they lay across the fretboard. Notice that most of the intervals are shown at least twice in each diagram, in order to cover multiple positions, but these are only alternate fingering choices; any duplicated interval notes are unison to each other.

Memorization of these charts now will make understanding scale and chord construction much easier when we get to those subjects later in this book.

Be sure to work through these charts with your guitar in your hand. You should practice jumping from the root note up to each interval, and say the names of the intervals aloud as you play them. Get used to the feel of these intervals in your hand (2 frets = Maj 2$^{nd}$; 1 string minus 2 frets = m3…), as well as their sounds. You can play these in any position along the neck. These aren't about any specific note names, just the relationships of pitches to each other.

**Top-left grid**

| | | | | |
|---|---|---|---|---|
| | | Maj 2nd | Perfect 5th | Octave |
| | | Min 3rd | Min 6th | |
| | | Maj 3rd | Maj 6th | |
| | Root | Perfect 4th | Min 7th | |
| | Min 2nd | Tritone | Maj 7th | |
| | Maj 2nd | Perfect 5th | Octave | |
| | Min 3rd | Min 6th | | |
| | Maj 3rd | Maj 6th | | |
| | Perfect 4th | Min 7th | | |
| | Tritone | Maj 7th | | |

**Top-right grid**

| | | | | |
|---|---|---|---|---|
| | | Maj 2nd | Perfect 5th | Maj 7th |
| | | Min 3rd | Min 6th | Octave |
| | | Maj 3rd | Maj 6th | |
| | Root | Perfect 4th | Min 7th | |
| | Min 2nd | Tritone | Maj 7th | |
| | Maj 2nd | Perfect 5th | Octave | |
| | Min 3rd | Min 6th | | |
| | Maj 3rd | Maj 6th | | |
| | Perfect 4th | Min 7th | | |
| | Tritone | Maj 7th | | |

**Bottom-left grid**

| | | | | |
|---|---|---|---|---|
| | | Maj 2nd | Tritone | |
| | | Min 3rd | Perfect 5th | Octave |
| | | Maj 3rd | Min 6th | |
| | Root | Perfect 4th | Maj 6th | |
| | Min 2nd | Tritone | Min 7th | |
| | Maj 2nd | Perfect 5th | Maj 7th | |
| | Min 3rd | Min 6th | Octave | |
| | Maj 3rd | Maj 6th | | |
| | Perfect 4th | Min 7th | | |
| | Tritone | Maj 7th | | |

**Bottom-right grid**

| | | | | |
|---|---|---|---|---|
| | | Min 2nd | Tritone | |
| | | Maj 2nd | Perfect 5th | |
| | | Min 3rd | Min 6th | |
| | Root | Maj 3rd | Maj 6th | |
| | Min 2nd | Perfect 4th | Min 7th | |
| | Maj 2nd | Tritone | Maj 7th | |
| | Min 3rd | Perfect 5th | Octave | |
| | Maj 3rd | Min 6th | | |
| | Perfect 4th | Maj 6th | | |
| | Tritone | Min 7th | | |
| | Perfect 5th | Maj 7th | | |

| | | | | |
|---|---|---|---|---|
| | | | | Min 3rd |
| | | | | Maj 3rd |
| | | | Root | Perfect 4th |
| | | | Min 2nd | Tritone |
| | | | Maj 2nd | Perfect 5th |
| | | | Min 3rd | Min 6th |
| | | | | Maj 6th |
| | | | | Min 7th |
| | | | | Maj 7th |

## COMPOUND INTERVALS

The intervals we've discussed so far have all been **simple** intervals; that is, they each sit within the range of one octave. Any intervals that are *larger* than an octave are known as **compound intervals**.

This isn't as tricky as it sounds. Because the musical alphabet repeats itself with every new octave, all you need to do is move the intervals you've already learned up another seven steps to the octave.

For example, the two frets separating C and D make that interval a major 2$^{nd}$. If you play the D an octave higher, keeping the C the same, that interval would be called a major 9$^{th}$.

By expanding any interval up an octave, you can find the compound intervals of 9$^{ths}$ (2$^{nds}$ + 7), 10$^{ths}$ (3$^{rds}$ + 7), 11$^{ths}$ (4$^{ths}$ + 7), and so on.

In the chart on the following page you'll see that that compound intervals all maintain the same major or minor quality as the simple interval they derive from: a *minor* 2$^{nd}$ up an octave is a *minor* 9$^{th}$; a *major* 3$^{rd}$ up an octave is a *major* 10$^{th}$.

## INTERVAL INVERSIONS

But what if the same two notes are flipped upside down, so that the note that was on top moves to the bottom? This is called interval **inversion**. So instead of these simple intervals:

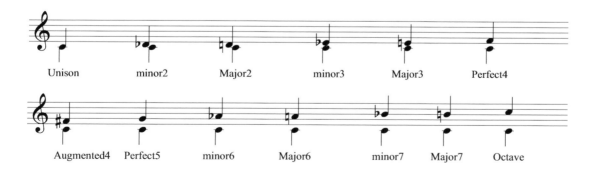

You would have these, the same notes, inverted:

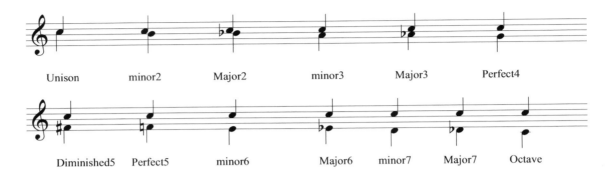

Unison      minor2      Major2      minor3      Major3      Perfect4

Diminished5  Perfect5      minor6      Major6      minor7      Major7      Octave

Notice that the distance from C up to E is a major $3^{rd}$. Those same two notes when inverted (C down to E) become a minor 6th. Likewise, C up to G is a perfect $5^{th}$, but inverted, C down to G, is a perfect $4^{th}$.

Interval inversion names can be calculated easily by remembering these two rules:

Rule 1: Major becomes Minor (and vice versa).

Rule 2: The sum of the two intervals is nine. For example, a major $3^{rd}$ becomes a minor $6^{th}$ (3+6=9).

---

The intervals of unisons, octaves, 4ths and 5ths are known as **Perfect Intervals**. They are called perfect because they are the intervals that are the most consonant, as opposed to the relatively dissonant major and minor sounds.

The perfect intervals of $4^{ths}$ and $5^{ths}$ can be made a half step wider (**augmented**), or narrower (**diminished**), and the resulting intervals will be considerably more dissonant than major or minor intervals. A perfect interval when inverted is still perfect, but diminished becomes augmented (and vice versa) and, like the other inversions, the sum of the two intervals will be 9.

---

# SCALES

## The Major Scale

The **major scale** is the most common **diatonic** scale used in Western music. The word diatonic means that the scale contains all seven letter notes within an octave.

Major scales are constructed following a regular pattern of major and minor $2^{nd}$ intervals, also known as **whole steps** (major $2^{nds}$) and **half steps** (minor $2^{nds}$). Remember that the distance from one fret to the next is a minor 2$^{nd}$ (half step), and two frets is a major 2$^{nd}$ (whole step).

The Major Scale pattern is:

Whole step – Whole step – Half step – Whole step – Whole step – Whole step – Half step

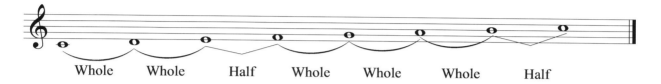

Like we did in the earlier interval lesson, we can illustrate this concept by using one string. Remembering that the guitar fretboard is laid out in half step increments, we can use this formula to play any major scale. Let's see how it looks using the fourth string:

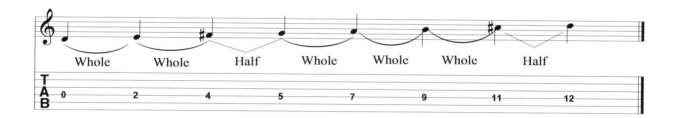

Play this example on your own guitar, and then explore ways to play other major scales starting on other root notes. First play the major scales starting on each of the open strings, then try starting from notes other than open strings. Just keep the "Whole – Whole – Half – Whole – Whole – Whole – Half" formula in mind and you'll be successful.

Practice saying the names of the notes as you play them: "D, E, F♯, G…." to reinforce the position of each note on the fretboard. Use the **fretboard** chart on page 28 of this book as a guide. Playing and spelling scales this way is a great way to learn your instrument.

Do not mix sharp and flat names in a single scale. Use either all sharps in your spelling, or all flats.

One last term to be aware of in the discussion of the major scale is **scale degree**. A scale degree, written as a number under a caret (ˆ), is the location of a pitch within the context of a scale. For example, the D in the D major scale shown above is scale degree $\hat{1}$ (also called the **root**), E is scale degree $\hat{2}$, F♯ is scale degree $\hat{3}$, and so on.

## Modes

Seven related scales, called **modes**, can be derived from the major scale. These carry Greek names and were used heavily in early Western music, like Gregorian chants. We have a couple of ways to understand the modes. One is to hear each scale degree of the major scale as a new tonal center. Treated this way, each mode will yield different melodic characteristics, despite being made of the exactly the same seven tones.

Sticking with the notes of the D major scale we played earlier, here are the seven related modes:

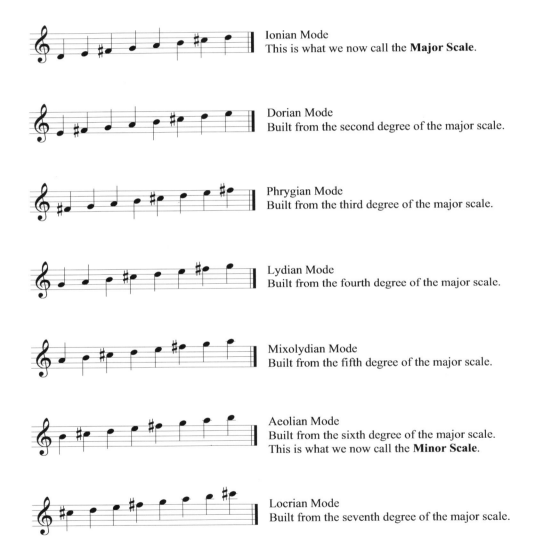

Ionian Mode
This is what we now call the **Major Scale**.

Dorian Mode
Built from the second degree of the major scale.

Phrygian Mode
Built from the third degree of the major scale.

Lydian Mode
Built from the fourth degree of the major scale.

Mixolydian Mode
Built from the fifth degree of the major scale.

Aeolian Mode
Built from the sixth degree of the major scale.
This is what we now call the **Minor Scale**.

Locrian Mode
Built from the seventh degree of the major scale.

Another, perhaps more useful, way to look at modes is to study how each mode is *different* from a major scale. Understanding the modes in this way allows improvisers to make quick changes between modes, without having to figure out the parent major scale of each mode.

The diagram below shows the seven modes that start from the note C. On the right of the diagram are scale construction notes based on how the modes deviate from the major scale.

The whole step/half step formulas we learned when we looked at the major scale are also shown below each mode. Pay particular attention to the fact that each mode still only has two half step intervals, and notice where those half steps occur within each mode. For example, the half steps in a Dorian mode are between scale degrees $\hat{2}$-$\hat{3}$ and $\hat{6}$-$\hat{7}$.

## Pentatonic Scales

**Pentatonic** scales are scales that contain only five notes. The Major Pentatonic is a five-note scale found by removing scale degrees $\hat{4}$ and $\hat{7}$ from the major scale.

**Major Pentatonic**

The minor mode of this scale, the Minor Pentatonic, is without doubt the most commonly used scale in rock music.

**Minor Pentatonic**

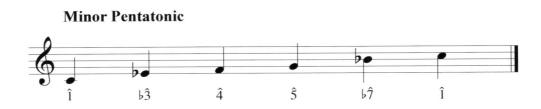

There's a common twist to the minor pentatonic scale, the addition of a tritone. When a $\flat\hat{5}$ is added to the minor pentatonic, you get the **Blues Scale**. Note that the $\flat\hat{5}$ note is only used as a **passing tone**, meaning you move through that pitch, rather than resting on it.

**Blues Scale**

Try to play these pentatonic scales by matching the scale degrees with the charts in *Appendix A: CAGED* on page 72. Each chart will have multiple fingering options. Find as many as you can and memorize them! Pay attention to the scale degree names as you play through the scales.

# HARMONY

## CHORDS

A **chord** is a simultaneous sounding of any three or more pitches, but obviously some combinations of notes will sound more consonant, and so find more frequent use, than others.

Now that we understand the basic units of intervals and scales, we can begin to understand how chords are built and used in Western music.

The basic unit of Western harmony is the **triad**. Triads are three note chords, built of stacked thirds. A triad is built from the **root** (the base of the chord), up the interval of a $3^{rd}$ to the **third** of the chord, and then up again another $3^{rd}$ to the **fifth** of the chord. So, for example, a Major triad would look like this:

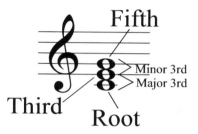

Working all the combinations of major and minor thirds yields four different types of triad: **Major**, **Minor**, **Diminished**, and **Augmented**. Here are their formulas:

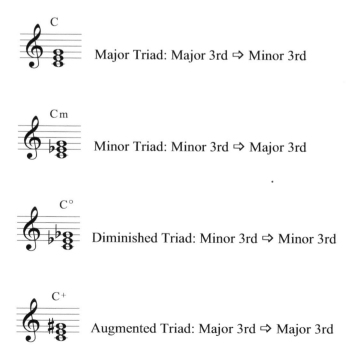

Notice also the size of the interval between the root and the fifth of each triad. The major and minor triads each have perfect 5ths, while the diminished and augmented triads feature diminished and augmented 5ths, respectively.

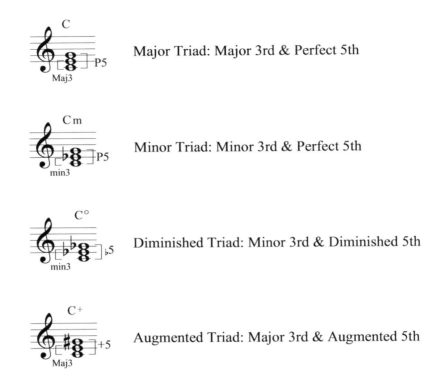

Major Triad: Major 3rd & Perfect 5th

Minor Triad: Minor 3rd & Perfect 5th

Diminished Triad: Minor 3rd & Diminished 5th

Augmented Triad: Major 3rd & Augmented 5th

**Note**: Remember that the diminished 5th is also known as a tritone. An **augmented 5th** is enharmonically the same as a minor 6th.

## Power Chords

One of the more common chords in hard rock and punk music is the **power chord**. Power chords, or 5 chords, are two note chords (**dyads**) made from a perfect 5th interval. Because they lack a third, they are neither major nor minor, and this contributes to making them easy to work with. The perfect 5th interval is consonant, so these chords work particularly well with heavily distorted guitar tones.

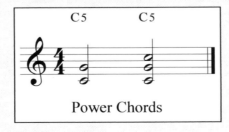

Power Chords

## Chord Inversions

Chords are spelled from the root up. So for example, a C major triad is spelled C, E, G:

But chords don't always need to be played with the root on the bottom. Any collection of C's, E's, and G's, regardless of order, will form a C major triad. A chord is **inverted** when a note other than the root is the lowest pitch. A **first inversion** triad has the 3$^{rd}$ of the chord on the bottom and a **second inversion** triad has the 5$^{th}$ on the bottom, but the same three notes are used in each chord.

Inversions like these are often written as **slash chords**. A slash chord is the name of the chord, followed by the name of the lowest note in the chord voicing. A C/E chord (spoken: "C over E") is, as in the example above, a C major triad with an E in the bass.

All inversions can be written as slash chords, but a slash chord does not necessarily have to be an inversion. Chords are often written as slash chords to show bass movement, and can include non-chord tones. One example is the C/D chord, a C major triad with a D bass note.

## Key

A **key** is a collection of notes, like the notes used in the major scale we played earlier, where one **tonic** (root) pitch serves as a tonal center, and all other pitches are subordinate to that tonic pitch.

These pitches have common names used to describe how each **scale degree** relates to the tonic. While the vocabulary here is useful when discussing scales with other musicians, more important is the insight the names provide about the way notes function in a key, and their implication that the tonic is the center of gravity for a key. Every note pulls in one way or another towards the tonic.

$\hat{1}$: *Tonic*: the first, and main note, of the key
$\hat{2}$: *Supertonic*: a second above the tonic
$\hat{3}$: *Mediant*: a third above the tonic
$\hat{4}$: *Subdominant*: a perfect fifth below the tonic
$\hat{5}$: *Dominant*: a perfect fifth above the tonic
$\hat{6}$: *Submediant*: a third below the tonic
$\hat{7}$: *Leading Tone*: a minor second below the tonic; or *Subtonic*: a major second below the tonic

## Diatonic Triads

We've learned about diatonic scales (scales that contain all seven letter notes within an octave), scale degrees, and triad chord construction. All three of these concepts come together when we talk about **diatonic triads**; which are chords made using the notes of a diatonic scale. For example, in the key of C, the diatonic chords are:

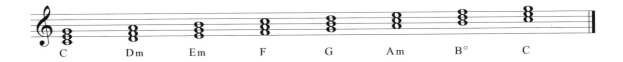

Chords, like single notes in a scale, are also called by scale degree names, but whereas single notes are written $\hat{1}$, $\hat{2}$, $\hat{3}$, $\hat{4}$, $\hat{5}$, $\hat{6}$, and $\hat{7}$, chords are written using **Roman numerals**: upper case for major triads and lowercase for minor triads.

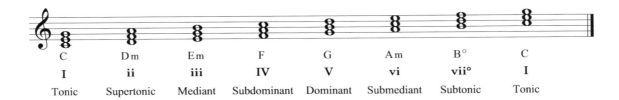

As was true for scale degrees, the advantage of knowing the scale position of each chord is in understanding how each chord functions within the key — how it fits relative to the tonic.

In a diatonic major key, the triads always follow a regular pattern of major and minor triads, and the Roman numerals reflect that. The pattern is: **I, ii, iii, IV, V, vi, vii°**. The uppercase **I**, **IV**, and **V** chords are major triads, while the lowercase **ii**, **iii**, and **vi** are minor triads. The subtonic chord is a diminished triad, and the symbol for a diminished chord is a small °, so the subtonic is written **vii°**. (See the earlier *Chords* section on page 39 if you need a review of these triads.)

The augmented triad isn't included here, because it isn't a diatonic chord. Augmented chords are covered later in the *Minor Keys* section on page 51.

As we continue this discussion of diatonic triads, I'm going to stop showing the triad built on the tonic octave in our examples, as it's simply a repetition of the first chord.

If we think again about the D scale, the one we played on the open fourth string in the Major Scales section, remember that the scale contained two sharps: F♯ and C♯. Here is that D Major scale again, minus the tonic octave:

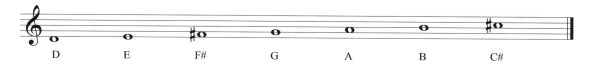

| D | E | F# | G | A | B | C# |

When we build triads on a scale we need to maintain the sharps or flats from the parent scale every time they occur, regardless of octave. With that in mind, the diatonic triads in D major will look like this:

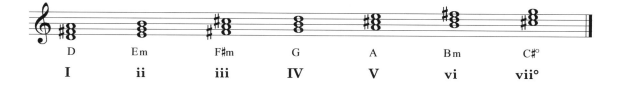

| D | Em | F♯m | G | A | Bm | C♯° |
| **I** | **ii** | **iii** | **IV** | **V** | **vi** | **vii°** |

Notice how the F♯s and C♯s are maintained throughout the example, but that the pattern of **I, ii, iii, IV, V, vi**, and **vii°** triads is the same as it was for the key of C major? The use of the accidentals (the sharps) might make this key look like it would be harder to play than the more simple looking key of C, but with the Roman numeral analysis you can see that the *patterns* within the key are all the same, and you begin to realize that one can approach all keys in the same way. This helps to demystify one aspect of music and lets you start approaching songwriting and improvisation in a fearless and intelligent way. There will be much more on this concept later in this book.

Having so many accidentals in your music does make for more complicated reading, however, and the solution is the use of key signatures.

## KEY SIGNATURES

The **key signature** is the group of sharps or flats at the beginning of a piece that indicates what key in which to play the song. This saves having to write out all the accidentals every time they occur, like we did in spelling out the chords in the key of D example earlier. The key of D major, we know, has two sharps, F♯ and C♯, so rather than writing this:

We could write the same thing more simply, using a key signature:

In the example above, the F♯ and the C♯ at the beginning of the staff is the key signature, and it instructs the performer to maintain those sharps through the entire piece.

The sharps or flats in a key signature affect *every measure and every octave* of the note. This makes them different from **accidentals**, which only last for the measure in which they occur, and only for the octave they are written in. Take the following short étude, for example:

It is not necessarily important for you to be able to play this example, just try to read it and understand which notes are sharp or flat, and what function the accidentals serve when they're used.

Here is that same example once more, but this time with some guidance:

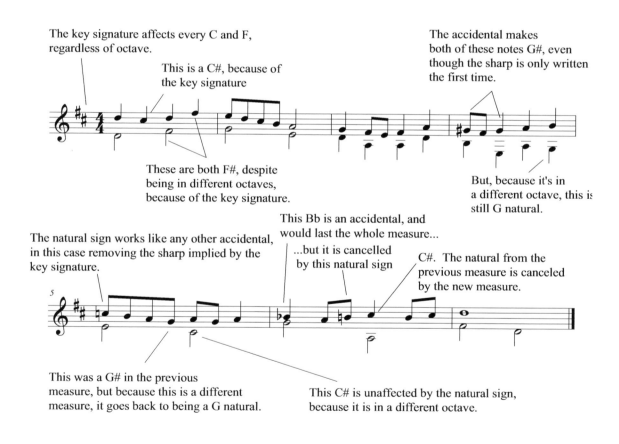

## THE CIRCLE OF FIFTHS

The **circle of fifths** is a powerful tool. It provides an easy way to see which notes belong to any key, relative major and minor key relationships, and key proximity relationships (helpful in modulations, discussed later).

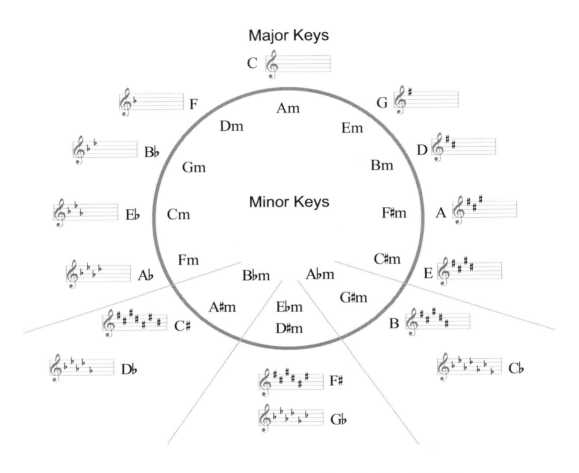

Around the outside of the circle you have a view of all the major keys, and inside, directly across from those major keys, are the **relative minor keys**. Notice that the name of the major key is six steps away from the name of the minor key (**C**, D, E, F, G, **A**)? That goes back to the minor scale being the Aeolian, or sixth **mode**, of the major scale, and that's why the two keys share the same key signature.

Three *rays* are at the bottom of the circle, each containing two seemingly different keys. These are **enharmonic keys**, meaning that although they are spelled differently — one made with sharps, one made with flats — they sound the same. This is the same principle we saw earlier when we learned that C♯ and D♭ are the same pitch on the guitar.

Below the Circle of Fifths we have the **order of sharps** and the **order of flats**. Sharps and flats always go in the same order: if a key has three sharps, they're F♯, C♯, and G♯. A key with five flats will have, in order: B♭, E♭, A♭, D♭, and G♭. You should commit the orders of sharps and flats to memory as soon as possible.

Let's use the circle of fifths now to find the notes in an E major scale.

1. Spell an E scale: E, F, G, A, B, C, D, E
2. Find the key of E on the Circle of Fifths
3. See that it has four sharps, and from the order of sharps you know that the four sharps will be F♯, C♯, G♯, and D♯
4. Add the sharps in the appropriate places, and you have your E major scale: E, F♯, G♯, A, B, C♯, D♯, E

E Major Scale

Now, apply the **I ii iii IV V vi vii°** pattern of diatonic chords to the E major scale and you'll find that the diatonic chords for the key of E are: E, F♯m, G♯m, A, B, C♯m, and D♯°.

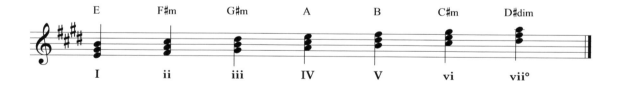

Let's try another one. The key of Cm has three flats. According to the order of flats, they are B♭, E♭, and A♭. So a Cm scale is spelled: C, D, E♭, F, G, A♭, B♭, C.

C minor scale

> Minor keys have some peculiarities that make working with them different from how we work with major keys. I will address them thoroughly in the following section on Minor Keys on page 51.

Push yourself to spell the scales of many other keys. The more you do this, the faster you'll get.

Another convenient feature of the circle of fifths is the quick view it can offer of the triads in a major key. Without going through the process we used above, you can just look at the circle itself and find six of the seven (the **vii°** chord is missing) diatonic chords.

Here's how to use the Circle of Fifths to find the diatonic chords, using the key of A (A, Bm, C#m, D, E, F#m, G#°) as an example:

1.  First find the **I** chord, in this case, A.
2.  To the left of the **I** chord (A), see the **IV** chord (D)
3.  To the right of **I** chord (A), see the **V** chord (E)
4.  Across from A, inside the circle, is the **vi** chord (F#m)
5.  To the left of the **vi** chord is the **ii** chord (Bm)
6.  To the right of the **vi** chord is the **iii** chord (C#m).

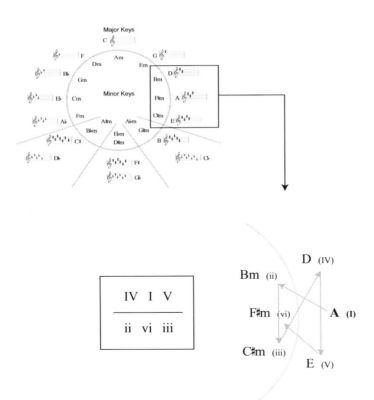

## Analysis Practice

Now that you can easily find the diatonic chords that belong to any major key, try looking through songs you enjoy, and see what chords they contain. Don't just look at the chord names, but also figure out what key the song is in and analyze the chord positions using the Roman numeral system.

As you work through analyzing your favorite songs, think about why the songwriter chose the chord movements they did. For example, many popular songs (*Let it Be* by The Beatles, and *Beast of Burden* by The Rolling Stones are just two) use a **I**, **V**, **vi**, **IV** chord progression. Other common chord progressions are **I**, **vi**, **IV**, **V** (*Stand By Me*, *Every Breath You Take*), or the classic blues form **I**, **IV**, **I**, **V**, **IV**, **I**, **V** (*Crossroads*, *Sweet Home Chicago*). What is it about those chord progressions that make them so usable? Why do *you* think they're so popular?

Getting familiar with the harmonic patterns of popular songs makes our work as guitarists and songwriters easier because it provides us with clues of where to look for chords in our own songs. For example, chord movements in fifths and fourths, like from **I** to **V** or **iii** to **vi**, sound great. And for the same reason, if you want to cycle back to a **I** chord, it's often best to use a **V** chord or **IV** chord to help you get there.

The more time you spend playing, listening to, and learning about chord movements, the more you'll find that it not only helps with original composition, but also aids with the transcription of other songs. If you've ever tried to figure out a song by ear, you know how tricky it can sometimes feel. Having this insight into what chords belong to a particular key, and knowing something about how chords typically fit together, makes the problem of figuring out the harmony of any song a more straightforward process.

Of course many songs will contain chords that don't fit perfectly into diatonic major keys, but don't worry. We're going to address those chords too, soon enough.

While seeing music in terms of diatonic keys helps us to identify certain patterns and musical clichés, most successful songwriters figure out ways of subverting those clichés so they can write music that sounds more fresh than familiar. I show you some tools you can use to recognize many of the non-diatonic chords used in popular songs, and show you how to apply those chords in your own songs, later in this book. But for now, experiment with different chord progressions using just the diatonic triads and listen to how the chords fit together. Explore!

## TRANSPOSITION

One last concept to address before we move on is **transposition**. Transposition is simply changing the key of a song to different key, like you do every time you use a capo. Numeric analysis makes it easy. As an example, a 12-bar blues in E can be written this way:

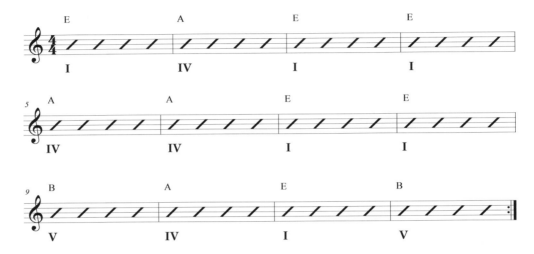

The analysis is already provided in the example above, shown with the Roman numerals below each chord. Let's change the key of this blues to the key of D.

Using the circle of fifths, we can find the chords for D, and then just substitute the original chords in E for the chord names in D that share the same scale degrees:

| E: | E | F#m | G#m | A | B | C#m | D#° |
|---|---|---|---|---|---|---|---|
| Degree: | **I** | **ii** | **iii** | **IV** | **V** | **vi** | **vii°** |
| D: | D | Em | F#m | G | A | Bm | C#° |

So our 12-bar blues, transposed to D, becomes:

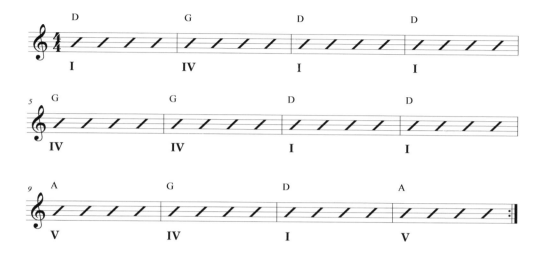

Roman numerals have been used for musical analysis like this for hundreds of years, but in the 1950s, studio musicians in Nashville developed a similar approach using Arabic numerals called the Nashville Number System. This system is discussed in *Appendix D: Nashville Number System* on page 78.

## MINOR KEYS

As we've seen, a **natural minor scale** is the sixth mode (the Aeolian Mode) of a major scale.

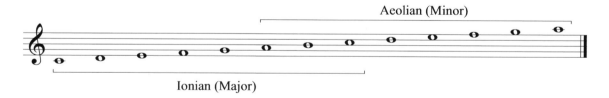

The pattern of triads (the three major triads, three minor triads, and one diminished triad) is likewise the same in the minor key as it was in the major key, but the numbers change to reflect that the tonic chord of the minor key is the former **vi** chord from the major key.

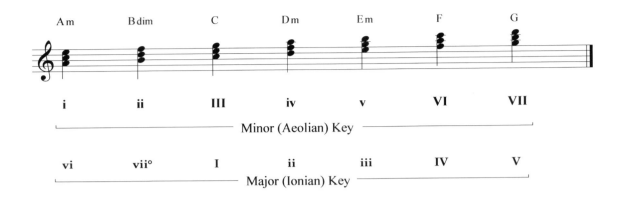

As you can see in the example above, this moves our major triads to **III**, **VI**, and **VII**; the minor triads to **i**, **iv**, and **v**; and the diminished triad now falls on the **ii°** chord. But, important to notice, the collection of chords is the same for both the major and relative minor keys.

Minor keys are slightly more complicated in practice, however, because in Western tonal music the **dominant** chord (the chord built on the fifth degree of the scale; the **V** chord) is nearly *always a major chord*. To do this in a minor key, we have to raise the third of the **V** chord a half step.

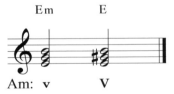

The reason the **V** chord tends to be major is that the tension and release that results from a **leading tone** resolving up to the **tonic** in a **V** to **I cadence** is such a powerful and desirable musical effect.

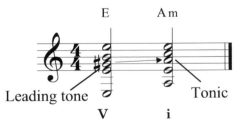

This leading tone resolution between **V** and **I** happens naturally in a major key, but in a minor key, we need to make this adjustment.

Incorporating the leading tone into a minor key this way gives us a new scale: the **harmonic minor**, so named because its origin stems from the harmonic improvement described above.

The interval between the $\hat{6}$ and the raised $\hat{7}$ scale degrees in a harmonic minor scale is called an **augmented 2nd** (enharmonically the same as a minor 3rd). This interval, which doesn't exist in any of the natural modes, gives the scale a vaguely Eastern European or Middle Eastern color, and is one of the coolest features of the harmonic minor scale.

Early composers found the augmented second melodically unacceptable, however, and so raised the $\hat{6}$ as well as the $\hat{7}$, giving us the **melodic minor** scale.

In classical music the melodic minor is played differently ascending than it is descending. An ascending melodic minor is, as above, played with the raised $\hat{6}$ and $\hat{7}$ tones, but when descending, the scale reverts back to the natural minor.

Composers treated the melodic minor scale this way because the raised $\hat{6}$ and the leading tone $\hat{7}$ generate strong upward momentum -- a need to resolve up to the tonic -- and that momentum makes descending melodic lines sound unpleasant. Returning to the natural minor on the descent solves the problem by lowering the $\hat{6}$ and $\hat{7}$ tones and restoring a descending feeling of motion.

Jazz musicians typically ignore this distinction and treat the melodic minor the same way both ascending and descending. When played this way, the scale is called the **Jazz minor**.

Another benefit of the harmonic and melodic minor scales is that a new sequence of triads can be built from the scales:

Triads built from the A Harmonic Minor scale

Triads built from the A Melodic Minor scale

Most of these chords are just our familiar major and minor chords, like we've seen in major keys, but notice the augmented triad, the **III+** chord. The interesting thing about that chord is that it is *almost never functionally used* as a **III+** chord, but rather almost always as a substitute for a **V** chord.

Why does it work to treat the **III+** as a **V+**? Augmented triads are **symmetrical chords**. That means any note in the chord can be treated as the root. So, just because the augmented triad happens to naturally occur in the **III+** position, it can also theoretically take the place of a **V+** or a **VII+**, since all three of those chords are spelled using the exact same three notes.

C, E, G♯　　　　E, G♯, B♯　　　G♯, B♯, D╳

(B♯ is the enharmonic equivalent of C)

(D╳ is the enharmonic equivalent of E)

As you can see above, a C+ chord is spelled C, E, G♯. If you take enharmonic equivalence into account, the E+ and a G+ chords are spelled exactly the same way, just inverted.

Remember, a **double sharp** (╳), like the D╳ in the G♯+ chord example above, raises a note by two half steps.

Be sure to play through the natural, harmonic, and melodic minor scales, and their respective diatonic triads. Use the interval charts and the fretboard chart to find the notes if you need to. Practice these things! Get them under your fingers and into your ears!

## Popular Harmony

Rock, pop, and country songwriters make infrequent use of dissonant chords like diminished and augmented triads. The most common method of avoiding a diminished triad, but still keeping a part of its leading tone flavor, is to use a **slash chord** (discussed earlier in the Chord Inversions section). Songwriters who want to have the leading tone sound of a chord, without the diminished chord dissonance, will often use a first inversion **V** chord to get it. In the key of C major this would be a G/B chord, or in the key of Am, an E/G#.

When doing an analysis of slash chords with Roman numerals, follow the Roman numeral by a slash (/) and use the **scale degree** of the note in the bass. For example, a second inversion G chord in the key of C would have this analysis: V/$\hat{7}$ because it's a **V** chord with the seventh scale degree, the B, in the bass.

Another common method of avoiding the dissonance of the diminished triad is by replacing it with a ♭**VII** chord. This is can be achieved by lowering just the root note of the existing **vii°** chord by a half step and playing the resulting major chord. This loses the leading tone tension, but is a common and interesting chord movement that you should explore. In the key of C major, the B° chord (**vii°**) would become a B♭ (♭**VII**) chord:

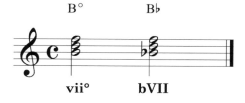

This leaves the typical songwriter with these commonly used chords:

Of these, it's the **I**, **IV**, **V**, and **iv** chords of the major key that are by far the most common.

Remember, it's the scale degrees (the Roman numerals) we want to focus on as the commonly used chords. The keys of C and Am are only shown above only as examples. The chord *relationships* work in any key.

## PARALLEL KEYS

We've talked at length about major keys and minor keys, although we've primarily discussed them as **relative keys** — modes of each other — as C is to Am, for example. **Parallel keys**, as in C to Cm, offer up further chord possibilities in songwriting and analysis. In the key of C, this offers the use of E♭, A♭, B♭, and G+ chords.

Many modern songwriters combine the chords from parallel keys with the relative keys, to take advantage of a large color palate with which to build their chord progressions. Adopting this approach, we could write a song in the key of C and feel free to use any of these chords:

You will find examples of chords being borrowed from the parallel minor key in a lot of songs. One particularly common example is the use of a **passing minor iv** chord in a major key.

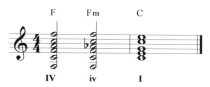

One reason this particular example sounds so good, is the chromatic motion in the inner voice of the chord: the way the third of the **IV** chord moves down a half step to the flat third of the **iv**, and finally resolves to the fifth of the **I** chord.

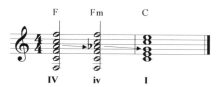

Adding this kind of chromatic **voice leading** is an effective way to build drama and harmonic interest into your music.

Pop and rock music often stays within established diatonic patterns, and augmented and diminished chords are not at all common in those genres. Borrowed chords from parallel keys are increasingly more common, but are still relatively rare when compared to the vast number of songs that use the **I**, **IV**, **V**, and **vi** chords exclusively. There are, however, plenty of hit songs that take advantage of a broader harmonic palette. A look through a Beatles songbook, as just one easy example, can be a revelation in the use of an extended harmonic reach. Stretch yourself and put these sounds in your own work! There are no rules. What sounds good, is good. These techniques are just tools to get your creativity flowing.

One way to explore this is by trying out all the possible options for the harmonization of a single note. Take the note C, for example. With just our knowledge of triads, we can treat that note as the root, third, or fifth of a chord. This yields a potential 10 triads that contain a C note.

Remember: augmented triads are symmetrical. The C in the C+ triad can be called the root (C+), third (A♭+, or enharmonically G♯+), or the fifth (F♭+, enharmonically E♭+).

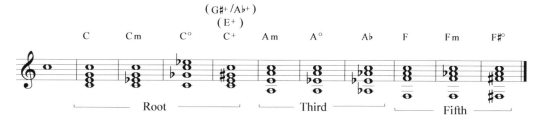

## Moving Beyond Triads

### Seventh Chords

Harmony based on intervals of thirds (**tertian harmony**) is the foundation of Western popular music and isn't limited to triads. If you stack another third above a triad, you get a seventh chord — so called because the note added is seven steps up from the root.

Seventh chords are the basic vocabulary of Jazz music, and they can be used to bring a taste of that sophisticated style to any song or genre in which you use them.

There are two seventh chords possible for each of our four previous triads, using either a major or minor seventh.

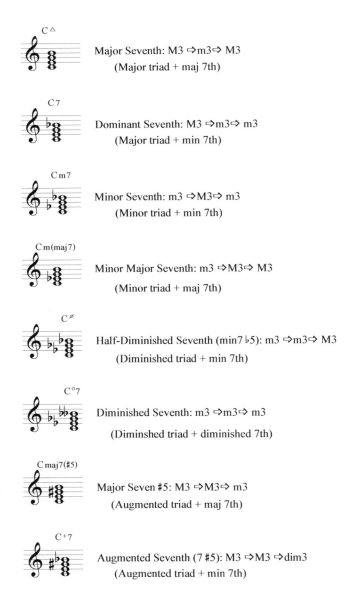

Major Seventh: M3 ⇨ m3 ⇨ M3
(Major triad + maj 7th)

Dominant Seventh: M3 ⇨ m3 ⇨ m3
(Major triad + min 7th)

Minor Seventh: m3 ⇨ M3 ⇨ m3
(Minor triad + min 7th)

Minor Major Seventh: m3 ⇨ M3 ⇨ M3
(Minor triad + maj 7th)

Half-Diminished Seventh (min7 ♭5): m3 ⇨ m3 ⇨ M3
(Diminished triad + min 7th)

Diminished Seventh: m3 ⇨ m3 ⇨ m3
(Diminshed triad + diminished 7th)

Major Seven #5: M3 ⇨ M3 ⇨ m3
(Augmented triad + maj 7th)

Augmented Seventh (7 #5): M3 ⇨ M3 ⇨ dim3
(Augmented triad + min 7th)

As we saw with triads, seventh chords line up in a specific way in a diatonic key.

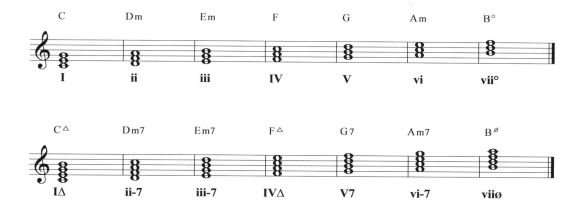

As we can see above, in a major key there are two **major sevens** (marked with a triangle, Δ) on **I** and **IV**; three **minor sevens** (marked with a dash, -) at degrees **ii**, **iii**, and **vi**; and one **half diminished** chord, also called a **minor 7♭5** (marked with a circle with a slash through it, ø) at degree **vii**.

For rock, blues, pop, and alternative music, however, the most common seventh chord is the one built off the fifth degree: the **Dominant Seventh**, marked with just a **7**). In a major key, there is only one dominant chord: at scale degree **V**.

## Dominant Seven Chords

The resolution of the leading tone to the tonic that makes a **V** to **I** cadence so desirable, as discussed earlier, is made even more forceful with a **V7** chord.

The key to the power of the **V7** to **I** cadence is the **tritone** interval between the third and the seventh of **V7** chord. The tritone is one of the most dissonant intervals in music, and as such, the resolution of that dissonance is one of the most powerful harmonic tendencies in Western music.

The typical resolution is to have the leading tone (the third of the **V** chord) resolve up to the tonic of the **I** chord, and the seventh of the **V** resolve down to the third of the **I**.

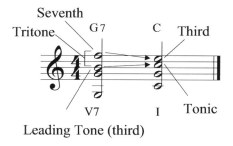

## MODULATIONS AND SECONDARY DOMINANTS

One method of developing harmonic interest in a song is through **modulation**, and dominant seven chords are a big help in that technique. Modulation is a key change that happens at some set point in a piece of music, often in a final chorus.

This can be as simple as playing the chorus chord progression up a half or whole step, as happens at the end of many pop songs, or it can be a subtle act — a series of chord movements that obscures for a time the original tonality until a new harmonic center becomes evident, almost without the listener noticing. This subtle technique is common in classical music, much less so in modern popular songs.

The trick to accomplishing a smooth modulation is to use a **common chord** — a chord from the original key that also exists in the new key being modulated to — as a bridge between the two keys. A common chord used this way is called a **pivot chord**. Say you were in the key of C and wanted to modulate to the key of F. Find the common chords between the two keys.

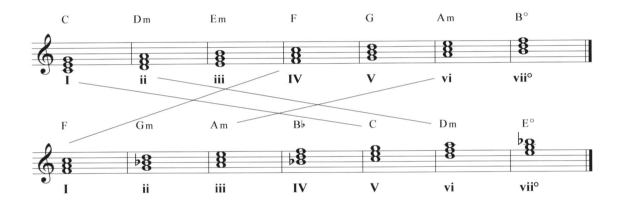

Here you can see that the C, Dm, F, and Am chords are in both the keys of C and F. You can use any of these common chords to pivot between the keys in your modulation, but since the **V** chord is the most effective at highlighting a new key, lets focus on the C chord, tonic in C and dominant in F.

To show the functional difference of the two C's as you begin to modulate, move from the triad to a dominant seven: from C to C7. The C7 in this case would be called a **secondary dominant**, a dominant seven pivot chord.

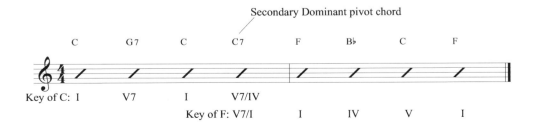

Secondary dominant chords also find their way into chord progressions that don't modulate, often as a tool to add emphasis to another chord, or just to shake up the sound of the chord progression.

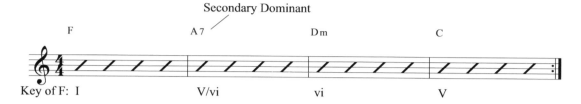

A secondary dominant chord is analyzed as, using the example above, **V/vi**, or "five of six". A dominant seven is always some kind of **V** chord, so when you see one in a song (other than a blues which almost always uses dominant seven chords exclusively), you need to think of it as borrowed from some other key. It's a **V** of *something*.

Here is a chord progression to play that makes extensive use of secondary dominant chords so you can see how effective they are at generating harmonic momentum.

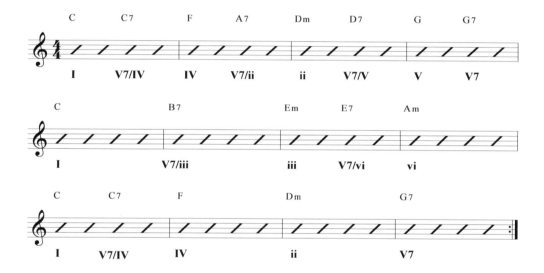

## COLOR CHORDS

### SUSPENSIONS

A triad is a three-note chord consisting of a root, a third, and a fifth. There are two other common three-note chords, called **suspensions**: the sus2 and sus4 chords. To play a "**sus chord**", simply substitute the third of a chord with either the second (sus2) or fourth (sus4) in a triad.

Suspensions are neither major nor minor, but can be used in place of either major or minor triads.

In the past there were specific ways to deal with suspensions; they get their name from an old counterpoint technique where the composer would "suspend" the interval of a fourth and resolve it down to a third. In modern harmony however, though the name persists, these have become stand-alone chords.

Most often, when a musician talks about a "sus chord", they'll be referring to a sus4 chord, not a sus2.

## add9 Chords

An **add9** chord is another common chord extension used to add color to major or minor triads. The add9 extension doesn't have a dramatic effect on the function of the triad, and isn't dissonant enough to require any special treatment, so use these wherever you think they sound good!

Be careful not to mistake an add9 for a major 9 or a 9 chord. An add9 chord does not have a 7th in the chord, while those others do. 9 chords (as opposed to add9 chords) are extensions that *must include the 7th*.

Moving the 9th of the chord down an octave, to a whole step above the root, turns the add9 chord into an **add2**. The add9 and add2 chords contain the same notes, but there is a voicing choice implied by the different names.

### ADD4 CHORDS

An **add4** chord is another colorful manipulation of a triad. The addition of the 4th to a major or minor triad has a dreamy effect, due to the dissonance of the 4th clashing with the 3rd of the chord.

Moving the 4th of the chord up an octave turns the add4 chord into an **add11**. The add4 and add11 chords contain the same notes and function the same way, but there is a voicing choice implied by the different names.

### SIXTH CHORDS

A sixth chord is yet another vehicle used to add color to a triad. These are major or minor triads with an additional note a 6th above the root. It's best not to invert 6th chords, as the inversions end up spelling m7 chords.

There are three types of 6th chord: the **major 6th** (a major triad with a major 6th), a **minor 6th** (a minor triad with a major 6th), and a **minor ♭6th** (a minor triad with a minor 6th).

### EXTENSIONS BEYOND THE SEVENTH

Extensions past the seventh, while adding a lot of color to a harmony, are considerably less common in rock, pop, and country music, and belong more to jazz harmony. A thorough explanation of all these chords is beyond the scope of this book. If you're curious about how best to use these extended chords, I suggest either *The Jazz Theory Book* by Mark Levine, or *Chord Chemistry* by Ted Greene.

That said, in rock music you can find plenty of 9 chords, 7#9 chords, and even some 13 chords, so it's important to know how to play those chords and to understand something about what they are.

As we've seen, by adding another interval of a major or minor third above a basic triad we gain a new and more complex chord: the seventh chord. Add another third above a seventh chord, and you have a ninth chord. Another third above that is an eleventh. Another third above that is the thirteenth.

These extensions add increasing complexity to the sound of a chord. Taken to the limit, basically any note from a scale can be understood to be some kind of chord tone. Here is a C major scale, stacked into a full CΔ13 chord.

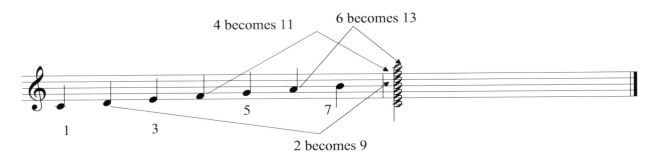

Obviously this seven-note voicing would be impossible to play on a six-string guitar, but it's shown here to illustrate the theory involved. With most extended chord voicings, you can leave out certain notes, the 5th in most cases is unnecessary. In the case of the CΔ13 above, by just playing the 1, 3, 7, 9, and 13, you would have enough harmonic content to hear the chord correctly.

There is something of an order of operations in the name of a chord. Once you understand that order, you can translate the name into a chord formula that will allow you to play or name any chord, so long as you know your intervals.

Here is how you read, or name, a chord, from left to right:

1. Root pitch of the chord
2. Seventh chord quality (major, minor, dominant, half diminished, diminished, or augmented)
3. The number of the highest extension note (♭9, 9, ♯9, 11, ♯11, 13)
4. Any special instruction (slash chord bass note, sus, any "add" notes, any important manipulations of the chord tones (♯5, ♭5, no 3rd…)

Not all of these elements will be used, obviously, for every chord, but generally, the more complex the voicing, the longer the chord name.

There is a list of formulas for many of the chords you will encounter as a guitarist in *Appendix B: Chord Formulas* on page 76 of this book.

## APPLYING MODES

With all this new harmonic information, let's look at some ways of using modes to build melodies or as tools for improvisations.

Look again at the construction of a dominant seven chord. We know that dominant seven chords are almost always some kind of **V** chord, so it stands to reason that the scale we would use to play over a **V7** would also be the fifth mode: the **Mixolydian** mode.

Choosing this mode insures we will have included all of the right chord tones in our scale. If your harmony is based solely on the tonic key (like most popular songs), and doesn't include any outside chords, the tonic scale works great and is all you need. But there are some interesting melodic choices you can make by exploring the sounds available from the other modes.

Here are the diatonic seventh chords in the keys of C major and C minor:

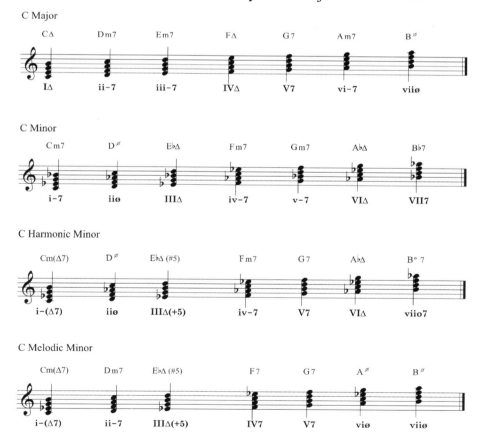

Looking back at our chart of diatonic seventh chords, you can see that dominant seven chords also show up as the **V** in the harmonic minor key, and as both the **IV** and **V** chords in a melodic minor key. That means that for a C7 chord, we can play melodic material based on, not only the Mixolydian mode like we saw above, but also the fifth mode of the F harmonic and melodic minor scales, and the fourth mode of the G melodic minor scale; the **Phrygian Major**, **Aeolian Major**, or **Lydian ♭7**, respectively.

See page 67 for a breakdown of the harmonic minor and melodic minor modes.

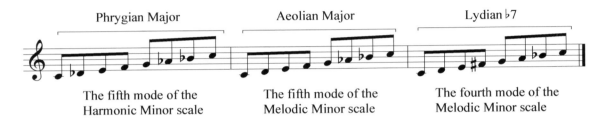

Phrygian Major — The fifth mode of the Harmonic Minor scale

Aeolian Major — The fifth mode of the Melodic Minor scale

Lydian ♭7 — The fourth mode of the Melodic Minor scale

You may notice that there is another dominant seven chord occurring as the **VII** chord in the natural minor scale, but because the natural minor is a mode of the major scale (from which we already drew our Mixolydian scale) it offers no new melodic content. That is why it is ignored here.

This same logic can be applied for the other common diatonic chord types:

| Chord | Usable Modes |
|---|---|
| Major | Ionian, Lydian, Mixolydian, Phrygian Dominant, Lydian #2, Lydian ♭7, Aeolian Major |
| Minor | Dorian, Phrygian, Aeolian, Harmonic Minor, Dorian #4, Melodic Minor, Phrygian ♮6 |
| Diminished | Locrian, Locrian ♮6, Alt Dominant ♭♭7, Locrian ♮2, Altered Dominant |
| Augmented | Ionian Augmented, Lydian Augmented |
| 6 | Ionian, Lydian, Mixolydian, Lydian #2, Lydian ♭7 |
| m6 | Dorian, Dorian #4, Melodic Minor, Phrygian ♮6 |
| m♭6 | Phrygian, Aeolian, Harmonic Minor |
| add9 | Ionian, Lydian, Mixolydian, Lydian ♭7, Aeolian Major |
| m (add9) | Dorian, Aeolian, Harmonic Minor, Dorian #4, Melodic Minor |
| Δ | Ionian, Lydian, Lydian #2 |
| -7 | Dorian, Phrygian, Aeolian, Dorian #4, Phrygian ♮6 |
| 7 | Mixolydian, Phrygian Dominant, Lydian ♭7, Aeolian Major |
| m7♭5 (ø) | Locrian, Locrian ♮6, Locrian ♮2, Altered Dominant |
| °7 | Alt Dominant ♭♭7 |
| mΔ7 | Harmonic Minor, Melodic Minor |
| Δ+5 | Ionian Augmented, Lydian Augmented |

Explore the melodic possibilities available with these scales! There are guides to finding fingerings for these scales and chords in the appendices of this book.

## HARMONIC AND MELODIC MINOR MODES

Just like we saw with the major scales, treating each note as a root can yield several additional scales, or modes. The harmonic and melodic minor scales are no different. Here are the modes of these minor scales.

Some of these scales have alternate names. Those names are shown in parentheses.

Harmonic minor modes:

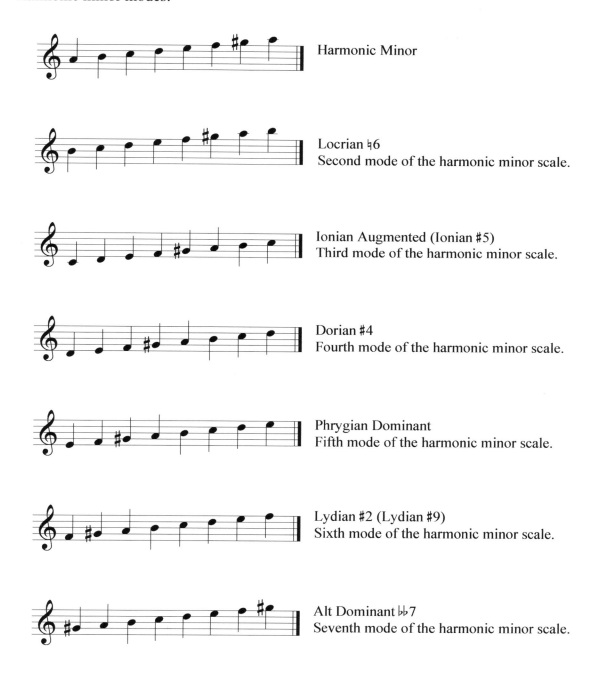

Harmonic Minor

Locrian ♮6
Second mode of the harmonic minor scale.

Ionian Augmented (Ionian #5)
Third mode of the harmonic minor scale.

Dorian #4
Fourth mode of the harmonic minor scale.

Phrygian Dominant
Fifth mode of the harmonic minor scale.

Lydian #2 (Lydian #9)
Sixth mode of the harmonic minor scale.

Alt Dominant ♭♭7
Seventh mode of the harmonic minor scale.

Harmonic minor mode construction formulas:

Melodic Minor Modes:

Melodic Minor

Phrygian ♮6
Second mode of the melodic minor scale.

Lydian Augmented (Lydian #5)
Third mode of the melodic minor scale.

Lydian ♭7
Fourth mode of the melodic minor scale.

Aeolian Major (Mixolydian ♭6)
Fifth mode of the melodic minor scale.

Locrian ♮2
Sixth mode of the melodic minor scale.

Altered Dominant (Super Locrian)
Seventh mode of the melodic minor scale.

Melodic minor mode construction formulas:

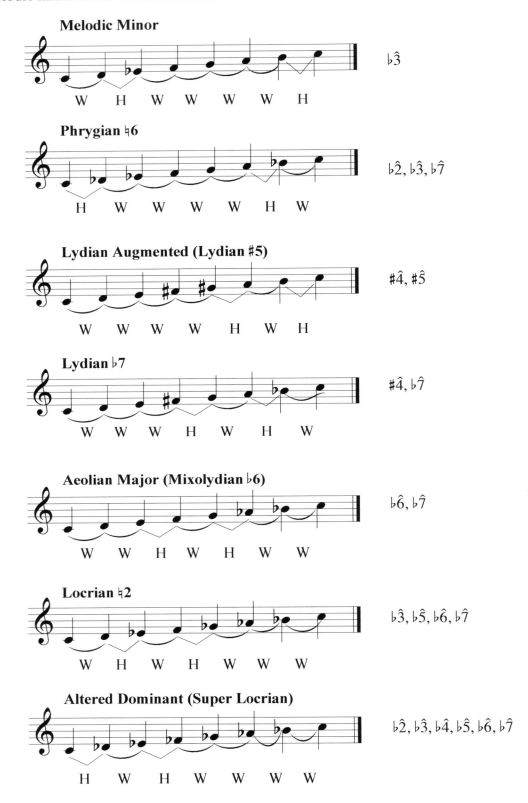

# WRAP UP

I have found that my students learn best when they take the formulas they learn and work out how to play the sounds on the guitar themselves. This usually leads to better retention and inspires creativity. My chief aim as a teacher has always been to develop and aid creative guitar players. We covered a lot of ground here, but I've intentionally not given many exercises or examples of how to use this information. Rather I hope you will dig in to this book with your guitar in your hand and explore all the possibilities yourself. I wanted this book to arm you with some new tools and provide you with some new ideas. Learning to apply all the concepts in this book is a lifetime's worth of practice and study.

Please visit my website at JustinSDavis.com. There you can contact me about any questions you have about this book, lessons with me, or strategies for using this book in your studio with your teacher or students.

Happy guitar playing!

# APPENDIX A: CAGED

The **CAGED** system is an effective visualization technique for guitar players. The name CAGED is an acronym made from the open position chords, and the barre chords that share their shapes. The roots of each chord are shown with diamonds.

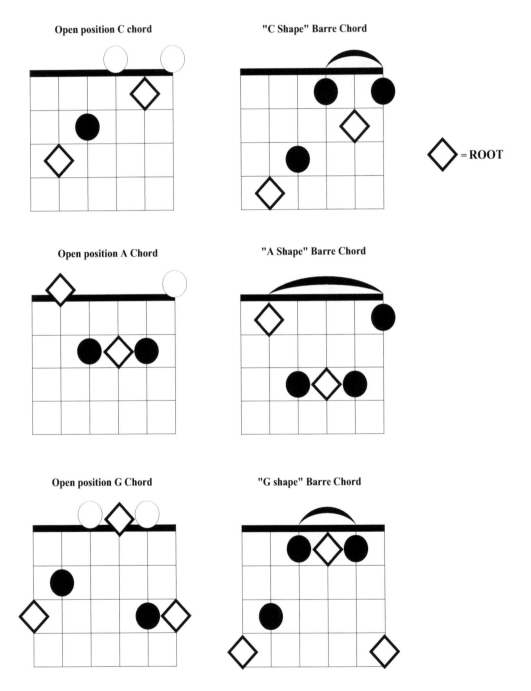

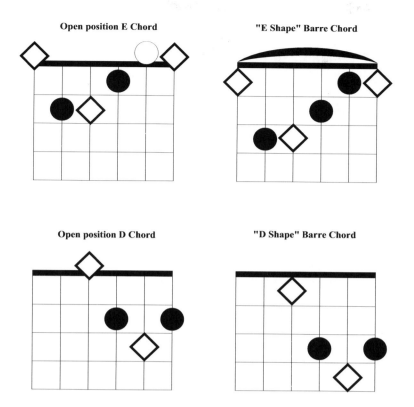

These five "shapes" interlock along the fingerboard in order with the acronym CAGED, so by learning the five shapes, you have access to the whole fingerboard.

In the following example, you see how the five CAGED boxes connect along the fingerboard. The key of C is shown as an example, but the way these boxes fit together is the same regardless of what chord you start with.

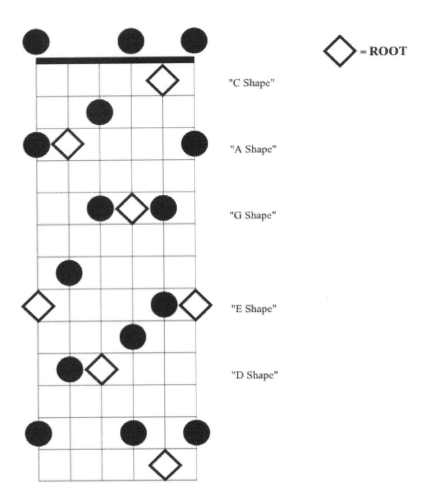

This sequence has powerful implications for learning the guitar. By familiarizing yourself with the way these roots fit together across positions, in the CAGED sequence, you can use a simple scale or chord formula and know how to play any scale, and any chord, anywhere on the fingerboard.

The charts that follow show the five CAGED shapes with interval names — with some compound interval names in parentheses for upper extension chords. Use the formula charts in *Appendix B: Chord Formulas* (chords) and *Appendix C: Scale Construction Formulas* (scales) to put these boxes to work for you. Master all the fingerings you can, and say goodbye to chord and scale dictionaries!

**"C Shape"**                    **"A Shape"**

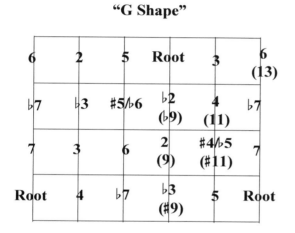 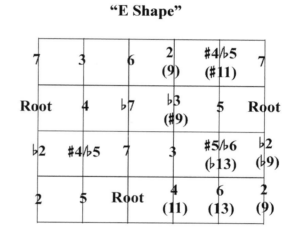

**"G Shape"**                    **"E Shape"**

**"D Shape"**

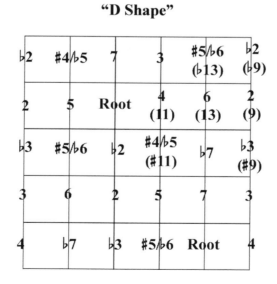

# APPENDIX B: CHORD FORMULAS

With some of these chords, it's impossible to play all the notes at once. *In most cases, you can leave out the 5 from the chord.* The non-essential chord tones are shown in parentheses. Use the CAGED interval charts in *Appendix A: CAGED* to find as many voicings of these chords as you can.

| Chord Type | Formula | Chord Type | Formula |
|---|---|---|---|
| **Power Chord** | | **Ninths** | |
| 5 | 1, 5 | add9 (add2) | 1, 3, 5, 9 |
| **Triads** | | m add9 | 1, ♭3, 5, 9 |
| Maj | 1, 3, 5 | 6/9 | 1, 3, (5), 6, 9 |
| m | 1, ♭3, 5 | m 6/9 | 1, ♭3, (5), 6, 9 |
| dim [°] | 1, ♭3, ♭5 | Δ9 | 1, 3, (5), 7, 9 |
| aug [+] | 1, 3, ♯5 | 9 | 1, 3, (5), ♭7, 9 |
| **Sus** | | 7♯9 | 1, 3, 5, ♭7, ♯9 |
| sus2 (2) | 1, 2, 5 | 7♭9 | 1, 3, (5), ♭7, ♭9 |
| sus 4 (sus) | 1, 4, 5 | 9♭5 | 1, 3, ♭5, ♭7, 9 |
| **Sixths** | | 7♭5♯9 | 1, 3, ♭5, ♭7, ♯9 |
| 6 | 1, 3, (5), 6 | 9sus4 | 1, 4, (5), ♭7, 9 |
| m6 | 1, ♭3, (5), 6 | m9 | 1, ♭3, (5), ♭7, 9 |
| m♭6 | 1, ♭3, (5), ♭6 | m9Δ7 (m9maj7) | 1, ♭3, (5), 7, 9 |
| **Sevenths** | | m7♭9 | 1, ♭3, (5), ♭7, ♭9 |
| maj7 [Δ] | 1, 3, 5, 7 | m7♯9 | 1, ♭3, (5), ♭7, ♯9 |
| 7 | 1, 3, 5, ♭7 | m9♭5 | 1, ♭3, ♭5, ♭7, 9 |
| 7sus4 | 1, 4, 5, ♭7 | **Elevenths** | |
| 7♭5 | 1, 3, ♭5, ♭7 | add4 (add11) | 1, 3, 4, (5) |
| m7 [-7] | 1, ♭3, 5, ♭7 | m add4 (add11) | 1, ♭3, 4, (5) |
| mΔ7 [m(maj7)] | 1, ♭3, 5, 7 | 11 | 1, 3, (5), ♭7, (9), 11 |
| m7♭5 [ø] | 1, ♭3, ♭5, ♭7 | m11 | 1, ♭3, (5), ♭7, (9), 11 |
| dim7 [°7] | 1, ♭3, ♭5, ♭♭7 | Δ7♯11 | 1, 3, (5), 7, (9), ♯11 |
| Δ7♯5 [maj7 ♯5] | 1, 3, ♯5, 7 | 7♯11 | 1, 3, (5), ♭7, (9), ♯11 |
| aug7 [+7] | 1, 3, ♯5, ♭7 | **Thirteenths** | |
| | | Δ13 | 1, 3, (5), 7, (9), 13 |
| | | 13 | 1, 3, (5), ♭7, (9), 13 |
| | | 13sus4 | 1, 4, (5), ♭7, (9), 13 |
| | | m13 | 1, ♭3, (5), ♭7, (9), 13 |

# APPENDIX C: SCALE CONSTRUCTION FORMULAS

These are the scales discussed in the book. Refer to the index if you want more information on any of these scales. Use the CAGED interval charts in Appendix A to find fingerings of these scales.

| Scale Type | Formula |
|---|---|
| Aeolian | See Minor |
| Aeolian Major (Mixolydian ♭6) | 1, 2, 3, 4, 5, ♭6, ♭7 |
| Alt Dominant ♭♭7 | 1, ♭2, ♭3, ♭4, ♭5, ♭6, ♭♭7 |
| Altered Dominant (Super Locrian) | 1, ♭2, ♭3, ♭4, ♭5, ♭6, ♭7 |
| Blues | 1, ♭3, 4, ♭5, ♮5, ♭7 |
| Dorian | 1, 2, ♭3, 4, 5, 6, ♭7 |
| Dorian #4 | 1, 2, ♭3, #4, 5, 6, ♭7 |
| Harmonic Minor | 1, 2, ♭3, 4, 5, ♭6, 7 |
| Ionian | See Major |
| Ionian Augmented (Ionian #5) | 1, 2, 3, 4, #5, 6, 7 |
| Locrian | 1, ♭2, ♭3, 4, ♭5, ♭6, ♭7 |
| Locrian ♮2 | 1, 2, ♭3, 4, ♭5, ♭6, ♭7 |
| Locrian ♮6 | 1, ♭2, ♭3, 4, ♭5, 6, ♭7 |
| Lydain ♭7 | 1, 2, 3, #4, 5, 6, ♭7 |
| Lydian | 1, 2, 3, #4, 5, 6, 7 |
| Lydian Augmented (Lydian #5) | 1, 2, 3, #4, #5, 6, 7 |
| Lydian #2 (Lydian #9) | 1, #2, 3, #4, 5, 6, 7 |
| Major | 1, 2, 3, 4, 5, 6, 7 |
| Major Pentatonic | 1, 2, 3, 5, 6 |
| Melodic Minor, ascending (Jazz Minor) | 1, 2, ♭3, 4, 5, 6, 7 |
| Minor | 1, 2, ♭3, 4, 5, ♭6, ♭7 |
| Minor Pentatonic | 1, ♭3, 4, 5, ♭7 |
| Mixolydian | 1, 2, 3, 4, 5, 6, ♭7 |
| Phrygian | 1, ♭2, ♭3, 4, 5, ♭6, ♭7 |
| Phrygian Dominant | 1, ♭2, 3, 4, 5, ♭6, ♭7 |
| Phrygian ♮6 | 1, ♭2, ♭3, 4, 5, 6, ♭7 |

# APPENDIX D: NASHVILLE NUMBER SYSTEM

In the 1950's studio musicians in Nashville developed a shorthand method of writing song charts using many of the principles we've learned from the Roman numeral analysis technique.

Basically, what they did was use the analysis as the primary chord name, instead of the chord's letter name.  This allowed for quick transposition in the (all too common) event of a singer needing a key change at the last minute.

Instead of Roman numerals, Nashville uses Arabic numbers, which means that instead of **I ii iii IV V vi vii°**, you would write **1 2m 3m 4 5 6m 7°**.  You also don't use bar lines in the Nashville system, as those can be easily confused with the number **1**, so every number you see lasts a full measure. If there are chord changes within a measure, those chords are **underlined** to indicate a split measure.

Here's a song, written in the standard chord notation as it would commonly appear in a lead sheet, followed by a Nashville Number example next to it. Compare the two sytems.

The Nashville Number System has given rise to some new vocabulary.  For example, the second line in the Nashville chart above would be called a "forty-four fifteen" because it's two measures of 4, followed by a measure of the 1 chord and a measure of the 5 chord.  Likewise, the last line would be a "fifteen eleven".  The split measures would be called a "split 6 minor, 6 minor over 5".

Now, we've seen how a measure with two chords can be split evenly with an underline, but what if the chords aren't evenly split?  Basic rhythm indications can be made with dashes over the chords for the number of beats each chord gets in a measure. So if a chord change occurs on beat four, for example, you could write the measure this way:

$$\overset{\text{...}\quad\text{'}}{\underline{1\ 5}}$$

Three chords in a measure can be split up the same way:

$$\overset{\text{..}\quad\text{'}\quad\text{'}}{\underline{1\ 4\ 5}}$$

Four chords in a measure evenly split can just be underlined:

$$\underline{1\ 6M\ 2\ 5}$$

The Nashville system also features some symbols that reflect other types of rhythms.  For example, a "diamond" is drawn around a number to indicate that the chord is to be struck and held, like a whole note:

A chord that is hit and quickly muted is marked with a "Dorito", a small filled in triangle over the chord:

A "push" rhythm, which is a chord moving on a preceding upbeat rather than the expected downbeat, as in this split bar:

is written with an accent mark over the pushed chord, like this:

Other specific rhythms can be notated under the measures. I like to keep the rhythms below an underline to show that the rhythm applies to that specific measure.  This works for both split measures and single chord measures, as shown below:

In split measures, take care to write the chord change directly above the rhythmic value where you want the change.  Here, the 4 chord happens over the first of the sixteenth notes:

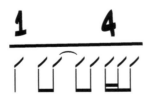

It is fine to use beat marker dashes for additional clarity:

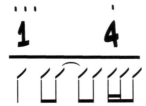

Time signatures are essential in the Nashville system because so much relies on knowing the beats of each measure, particularly when all you have to go by is the chord's scale degree.  If you need to change time signatures for a section of a tune, you can do that in a few ways.  I like putting the measure in parenthesis and marking with dashes the number of beats in that measure, but that only works if the note value getting the beat is the same as the rest of the tune (a measure of 3/4 in an otherwise 4/4 tune, for example).

Here you see a 4/4 measure (indicated by the time signature) starting on the 5 chord, followed by a measure of 1 in 3/4 time, and returning to 4/4 for the next 5 chord:

$$\tfrac{4}{4})\ 5\ \overset{\cdots}{(\,1\,)}\ 5$$

If the basic value of the beat changes, however, you need to indicate that.  The trick is to make sure the new time signature can't be confused with a slash chord.  Many people manage this by drawing a box around each affected measure and putting the new time signature inside parentheses:

$$\tfrac{4}{4})\ 5\ \boxed{(\tfrac{6}{8})\,1}\ 5$$

In the example above, only the 1 chord would be played in 6/8 time, the 5 chord that follows would go back to 4/4. If there were many measures in the new time signature, you'd put boxes around each one.

Here is a short Nashville chart etude that uses many of these elements. See if you can play your way through it.

(KEY OF G)

Hopefully, this is enough information that you could look at a basic Nashville chart and play through it, but bear in mind that the Nashville system is still relatively young and isn't totally standardized.  Depending on the preferences of the person writing the chart, Nashville charts can have many different looks to them. For example, some people prefer to draw boxes around measures with specific rhythms, instead of writing them under an underline. The information provided here will get you close, but isn't intended to be an exhaustive presentation.

If this system is interesting to you, and you want to dig into it further, I recommend the excellent book, *The Nashville Number System* by Chas Williams, which breaks down these elements thoroughly and features many pages of Nashville charts written by studio pros.

# *Manuscript Pages*

# INDEX

WARD STREET PRESS
SEATTLE, WASHINGTON

WWW.WARDSTREETPRESS.COM

Made in the USA
San Bernardino, CA
16 September 2016